LIGHT FOR THE JOURNEY

LIGHT FOR THE JOURNEY

Living the Ten Commandments

ERNEST J. LEWIS

WORD BOOKS
PUBLISHER
WACO, TEXAS

A DIVISION OF
WORD, INCORPORATED

Library of Congress Cataloging in Publication Data

Lewis, Ernest J., 1927–
    Light for the journey.

    1. Ten commandments.   I. Title.
BV4655.L43   1985   241.5'2   85–17968
ISBN 0–8499–0393–9

Printed in the United States of America

6 7 8 9 8 BKC 9 8 7 6 5 4 3 2 1

To
Jean, Kathy, Michael and *Steve*
my family and the most important people in my life

Acknowledgments

First to W. Clement Stone, whose trust, encouragement and inspiration made this book possible. Also with special appreciation to Mary Belfield, whose early help planted the seeds of this book a decade ago; to Dick Skinner, whose sharing of his daily application of these commandments kept the idea of a book on the back roads of my mind; to Dorothy O'Neal, my personal secretary, whose faithful hundreds of hours of typing, proofreading and typing over again have made it all happen. Her steady friendship, together with the friendship and practical help of her husband, Don, has also been the assuring influence throughout; to the friends and colleagues who, over the years, have encouraged me to write. Sincere and heartfelt thanks to all and to each.

The suggested discussion questions were added using W. Clement Stone's formula: to *recognize, relate, assimilate* and *apply* principles to achieve one's goal. In this case, the goal is discovery and fulfillment which God wants to give to us in the joyful keeping of his commandments, his *Light for the Journey*.

"Hear, O Israel: The LORD our God is one LORD; and you shall love the LORD your God with all your heart, and with all your soul, and with all your might. And these words which I command you this day shall be upon your heart; and you shall teach them diligently to your children, and shall talk of them when you sit in your house, and when you walk by the way, and when you lie down, and when you rise" (Deut. 6:4–7, RSV).

Contents

Foreword

Your two greatest powers to achieve success in any worthy endeavor are:

1. The *Power to Choose* and
2. The *Power of Prayer.*

It's wonderful to teach the Ten Commandments. But Dr. Ernie Lewis and I have often discussed a dilemma: A person may memorize the Ten Commandments yet—because of inherited primitive instincts, passions, emotions, moods, tendencies, etc.— not know how to motivate himself to live up to them. That individual may not truly understand the meaning of that which he has committed to memory. If living in accordance with God's guidelines is one of your goals, Ernie has GOOD NEWS for you!

I met Ernie when he became pastor of the First Presbyterian Church of Evanston. He has a wonderful talent for bringing to life characters and concepts from the Bible and proving the contemporary nature of *The Word.* Our friendship has matured through the years and we have learned much from each other. We have often shared the speaker's platform . . . Ernie on Religion, and I on the Art of Motivation with PMA (Positive Mental Attitude).

Many years ago, after reading *The Magnificent Obsession* by Lloyd C. Douglas, I developed a magnificent obsession of my own . . . a burning desire to *change the world and make it a better world for this and all future generations.* When you have a major definite purpose and keep your mind on it constantly—actually *live* it—you are apt to recognize opportunities and take actions that will, step by step, help you achieve it. I recognized an important and powerful principle in John Donne's immortal lines, "No man is an island, entire of itself; every man is a piece of the continent." To achieve my magnificent obsession, my mission in life, I must multiply myself with talented, dedicated, experienced persons . . . form mastermind alliances with such persons, working in harmony toward the goal of making this a better world. I have been fortunate to learn from and work with leaders in government, business, education, religion, welfare and volunteer programs the world over. Together, we are achieving that which no one of us could do alone. Ernie Lewis is an important member of my mastermind alliance.

My expertise as a writer, lecturer and educator is to motivate individuals to learn and apply two principles that were never taught in the history of education. They are: (1) how to *Recognize, Relate, Assimilate and APPLY* principles from what you see, hear, read, think or experience and from other disciplines so as to achieve any goal whatsoever that doesn't violate universal law—the laws of God and the rights of your fellowman (I call this my *"R2A2*

Formula"); and (2) how to use your conscious mind to tap the unlimited power of your subconscious to achieve any worthy goal.

The electronic computer was designed to function similar to your brain and nervous system—your human computer. You feed the electronic computer data and formulas and it solves problems with speed and accuracy. But you never get out of the computer more than you take the time to put into it. So it is with your human computer. Therefore, keep an open mind.

Throughout the history of education, you could get a diploma at any elementary or high school, or a degree in the behavioral sciences at any university or seminary primarily by using your memory—feeding your human computer data to create an information bank. But you may never have recognized principles that could figuratively put the true riches of life and the wealth of the world in the palms of your hands. This is where the R2A2 Formula comes in! With the right formula, your human computer will work more quickly and efficiently to provide you with answers you may seek.

I guarantee you success if you will engage in thirty minutes each day of creative thinking time. Write on the cover of a notebook "How I Can Achieve ANY Goal." On one of the pages, write your worthy, long-term goal . . . to live the Ten Commandments. Each day, without fail, in a quiet environment where you won't be disturbed, look at and concentrate on your goal. As thoughts come to your mind, jot them down—ideas that may be helpful in one column, obstacles to be overcome in another. Through repetition, repetition, repetition . . . your subconscious will come up with the answers you are seeking.

Remember: The essence of perfection is never reached . . . but you become more perfect by striving to live the Ten Commandments.

W. Clement Stone

1

CHOICES

Mark Twain had a friend who often led groups to the Holy Land and then on to Mount Sinai where God gave the Ten Commandments to Moses. One day he said to him, "I wish instead you would stay home in Boston and teach people how to obey the commandments there."

In his typical crusty style, Twain made his point clear. As he saw it, there was far more to be gained if people would stay home and obey the Ten Commandments than run halfway across the world to visit the spot where they were given. Twain implied that society of his time was in dire need of the regulatory values inherent in the Ten Commandments. But if that was true then, it is even more so today. We are experiencing a growing uneasiness, bordering on despair, as we try to sort out what is right and wrong. That uneasiness is accompanied by a hunger for something or someone we can trust. We need something or someone who will show us how to cope with the complexities of our relationships within the family and the church, and with our neighbors around the world. We sense a need for more than just information and abstract guidelines.

Ten Rules for Living

I believe that God anticipated our need more than three thousand years ago when he gave us his ten rules for living—the Ten Commandments. Unfortunately, they have become so familiar to us that we no longer *hear* what God is saying to us through them, and thus we miss the electric impact of their message. In addition, we tend to rebel, consciously or unconsciously, against the "thou shalts" and the "thou shalt nots" because of our permissive nature. Instead of seeing these words of the Lord as a deep expression of his love and as a pathway to freedom and wholeness, we get caught up in negatives. We become careless with overfamiliarity of the commandments.

But God is not a killjoy. These commandments were not given to limit our freedom or focus on punishment. Instead, they point the pathway to purposeful living and fulfillment. The same God who gave them to us spoke through Jesus when he said, "I have come that you might have life, and have it more abundantly." In the Ten Commandments we have, in reality, rules for love and relationships that lead us to responsible behavior. They lead us to a loving relationship with God and each other, to acceptance and affirmation of ourselves as children of God.

This is why a new and fresh look at the Ten Commandments will lead us to an adventure in living that is exhilarating and freeing. In them we have direction for making right choices, for it is the choices

17

we make in life that affect our happiness or unhappiness. It is the drama of our "yes" and our "no," our freedom and its consequences, that determine our closeness to God and each other and our feelings about ourselves. God's commandments and our responses to them are basic to the quality of life we are living at any moment.

Edwin Markham put this eloquently into verse:

> When in the dim beginning of the years,
> God mixed in man the rapture and the tears,
> And scattered through his brain the starry stuff,
> He said, "Behold, yet this is not enough,
> For I must test his spirit to make sure
> That he can bear the vision and endure.
> I will leave man to make the fateful guess,
> Will leave him torn between the no and yes,
> Leave him unresting 'til he rests in Me,
> Drawn upward by the choice which makes him free.
> Leave him in tragic loneliness to choose,
> With all in life to win or all to lose.[1]

Living in Relationships

God's commandments also teach us about the nature of life itself as he created it to be. They teach us that God created us for relationships, and our deepest moments are lived out in relationships. That's why the Ten Commandments are as vital today as they were when Moses received them on the mountain. They keep pointing us to God and to each other. Though we have changed our methods of transportation, our style of dress, our energy sources and thousands of other things, we still need to love and be loved. We still need to learn to forgive and be forgiven.

I'll always remember when our oldest daughter, Kathy, was a teenager. She would "prowl" late at night, washing and fixing her hair or doing any one of a hundred things that teenagers do. One night late, too late, I heard her in the upstairs hall and shouted, "Get thee to bed. Now!" A scurry of bare feet and a hastily closed bedroom door convinced me she had heard and obeyed! But then later when her mother and I went to bed, we felt more than a little guilty as we read the handmade Valentine taped to our bedroom door that said, "I Love You."

Yes, love, joy, peace and happiness come as our choices and decisions are centered in God. The Ten Commandments help us gain an understanding of what God is like and what he desires. God spoke clearly on Mount Sinai. In those memorable words we find none of the complicated theological jargon that so often fogs the atmosphere on Sunday. As we choose to listen, the Word of God will come through clearly in these commandments so that we see beyond the commandments to the Commander; beyond the law to the Lawgiver. And *in* the Lawgiver, we discover the life he wants us to enjoy in the fullness of relationships.

Making Right Choices

Then in addition to giving us a clearer understanding of what God is like, the commandments teach

19

us something about what it means to be human. This is important if we are to make right choices for we humans are unique in all of God's creation in our ability to choose. The Psalmist makes it clear that God's marvelous and awesome creation unites to sing his praises. "The heavens declare the glory of God; and the firmament sheweth His handiwork" (Ps. 19:1). Every star and every cricket sings God's praise. But the amazing fact is that while the rest of creation can praise God, only humans can *disobey* God. *It is human disobedience that produces dissonance in God's song of creation.* Because only humans can disobey God, only they can really obey God as a response of willing choice. Locked within our possibilities are both obedience and disobedience. And the response of our willing choice finds its outward expression not only in what we say but in our *actions* either of willful obedience to God or of disdain, indifference or ignorance.

Playwright George Bernard Shaw once observed that he knew what people believed not by their creeds but by "the basic assumptions upon which they habitually acted." What we *do* most clearly reveals what we believe.

The Ten Commandments are built upon the very foundations that affect our personal lives. From them we learn that we are free to choose. But we learn also that the exercise of that freedom has consequences. We are free to say yes or no to God, but our lives reveal the consequences of those choices.

20

Who Is Breaking Whom?

Even though we are free to choose, no one really breaks the Ten Commandments. If we are disobedient, they break us. They are not God's ten suggestions! We live in a universe governed by laws. It is God's universe and it is his law. In the physical world, we are quite familiar with this. If we step off the edge of a roof, we will fall victim to the law of gravity.

In our scientific and technologically oriented age, we recognize with precision that one must take into account every law in the natural universe to plant an object on Mars or on the moon. If we vary, if we choose to ignore those laws or misread them, we have to settle for failure. We miss the goal. We simply cannot accomplish our purpose.

By the same token, there are moral and spiritual laws that must be followed or we will fall victim to their consequences. It is still true that "the soul that sins shall die." And it is equally true that "love never fails." For every action there is a reaction.

That same sovereign God put within our moral and spiritual lives some guides by which we can find freedom and love and meaning and purpose. Look at the commandments. Note their direction. The first four steer us directly to God. We begin with our relationship with him. So we talk about God's being, God's worship, God's name, God's day.

And the last six point us toward society—toward our neighbor. Our neighbor's name, his reputation, our neighbor's goods—thou shalt not steal them. Thou shalt not even want them with greed. Don't *covet* them. Don't kill. Your neighbor's life is precious. As Jesus interpreted it, your neighbor is every other human being on earth. Just like the horizontal and the vertical hold on television, we don't get the picture until we see God reaching out to us in the law, in both directions—to himself and to each other.

In our late twentieth-century world the words *commandment* and *law* don't strike a responsive chord. They sound "bossy," and we don't want to be bossed. Authority is suspect; we want to live according to our own set of rules. Robert Nesbitt has observed that the Western world has cut itself loose from any acknowledged authority in most of the traditional disciplines and areas of our lives, and that this phenomenon is new in our long cultural history. Yet, in spite of this urge, there is an inner hunger for some authority that we can trust.

It's almost as if we have driven the wrong way on a one-way street, come to a dead end and wonder what signs we missed along the way. Recently, I read that somewhere in Florida some mischievous teenagers had pulled up the stop signs along a stretch of road and had thrown them into the thick palmetto bushes. Two cars, traveling at high speed, crashed and several people were seriously injured. This tragic accident occurred simply because two important signs had been removed.

Road Signs Are Needed

In many ways the Ten Commandments are like those road signs. We need them if we are to avoid the destructive crashes at the crucial intersections of life.

Not long ago, I flew to a southwestern city for several days of conferences. I was met at the airport by an old friend, a welcome sight in the midst of all the confusion and people at the airport. After claiming my baggage, we walked across to the parking ramp and climbed into a sleek, black Mercedes Benz. As we moved out into the heavy afternoon traffic, he looked over at me and said, "Ernie, this car is yours to use while you are in Dallas."

I spent the next few minutes asking questions about how to operate the car. To me, its dashboard looked like the cockpit of a small airplane.

The next morning I climbed into this technological wonder with more than a little anxiety, but I pushed all the right buttons and everything went beautifully. I zipped around from appointment to appointment as if I had driven a Mercedes all my life, and my confidence and satisfaction were high as I returned to the hotel late that afternoon.

After a leisurely dinner, I headed back to the hotel parking lot to get the car. It was pitch dark and I fumbled around, trying to find out how to turn on the lights. After two or three minutes of turning knobs and pushing buttons, and still no lights, I began to get frantic. In desperation I fumbled through the glove compartment in search of an operations manual, but with no success. All I could find was an invoice that told me the car had cost $32,367.

Turning back to the dashboard, I kept fumbling with knobs and buttons and learned how to slide the sun-roof back and forth, move the seats to six positions, raise and lower the windows, lock the doors, operate the windshield wipers and washer. I located the radio and tape deck controls and even pushed a button that caused hazard signals to flash in bright orange—but no lights! There I was in a $32,000 car and I couldn't go where I needed to because I wasn't able to find the light switch.

In this complex world of ours, the Ten Commandments are our light switch in a dark and confusing society. They are, as John Calvin said, "a lamp to guide our feet" if we will only choose to obey them. They were meant to be *Light for the Journey*. Part of the majesty and mystery of our humanity is that God created us capable of choice, and he wants us to choose life by choosing him, his way and his will.

But the choice is always ours.

Questions

1. Use this time to become acquainted with each other. Go deeper than just names and occupations. (As a child, what is your first memory of *thinking* about God? And share how you *felt* about God as a child.)
2. Share at least one thing you hope to gain from this book and discussion time.
3. Name at least one central idea that seemed important to you from this first chapter.
4. Can you name one thought from this first chapter that could change your life?

2

GOD'S PRIORITY

Thou shalt have no other gods before me.

Exodus 20:3

While in the New Testament we are told to seek the kingdom of God, the Old Testament says we should seek the King. This commandment is primary. It commands simply and directly—put God *first*. For God's kingdom to be first in our lives, God the King must be first. The first commandment states it clearly: "Thou shalt have no other gods before me."

This was an important commandment at the time it was given because the Hebrews lived among people who worshiped many gods. But it is equally important for us today, because while we pay lip service to one God, we so often put other things and other people ahead of him. They become our gods.

I remember very well things and people that took first place in my youth. After the football season of my high-school junior year, several of my teammates and I enlisted in the U.S. Marine Corps. World War II was at its peak and I was seventeen years old. My mother's heart almost broke when I enlisted, but my dad seemed to understand. I spent three years in the Marines, and came out of it much wiser in the way of the world, but not a Christian.

Love at First Sight

I was twenty years old when I returned to high school, and that's when I met lovely, vivacious, seventeen-year-old Jean. It was love at first sight for me! But it wasn't for her, because she wasn't ready to settle for just one man in her life. After graduation from high school, we went to separate colleges, but I was still sure she was the one. Unfortunately, she wasn't ready to make a commitment to me. Jean was a Christian but I wasn't, so the real battle between myself and God took place that first year in college.

God wanted to be first in my life, before everything and everyone else, even Jean. And God worked me over pretty good!

My battle took place one cold night in early November. My heart and soul were in turmoil. I wandered for hours along country roads outside the college town and through wet and chilly fields. I prayed not even in sentences, but with all my heart and my very being. Finally, I ended up alone in my room, on my knees, with scalding tears running down my cheeks. I was ready to give my whole life to God. Everything for all time. Well, almost everything. Everything but Jean. I just couldn't think of losing her.

I didn't know much about the Bible and nothing about theology, but I knew I needed cleansing and I needed God. But wanting Christ more than Jean was the pivotal point. Finally, this 220-pound, six-foot-four-inch ex-Marine sobbed out the words,

"Okay, God, even Jean. I even give my love for Jean to you." And you know what? God in his compassion gave me a deep sense of peace, and I went to bed and slept the quiet sleep of the redeemed.

But the story doesn't end there. As I write this, Jean and I have been married thirty-six years. But the real miracle happened the night I sobbed my way into salvation. Shortly after, Jean wrote me a letter from hundreds of miles away telling me of her love and acceptance, and we became engaged that next December. We were married a year later and struggled together through the rest of college and graduate school and through the good times and the hard times that have been a part of our years together. It all happened, I'm convinced, because I put God first, fighting all the way, and gave my life to him. Then and only then he trusted me with the desires of my heart.

Who Is Your God?

People and things can become gods that come before our love for God. He won't take second place, and why should he? He is sovereign, majestic, Lord of all!

When God says in Exodus 20:2–3 (RSV), "I am the LORD your God, who brought you out of the land of Egypt, out of the house of bondage. You shall have no other gods before me," he is saying something profound and yet very personal. If God had said, "I am the One who is creator of the world," that would have been significant, but very general. Yet, the meaning is so much deeper when he begins by saying that he is the God who led *you* out of Egypt. The Hebrew word for "you" is a singular pronoun, so in reality he is saying to each individual person that he is the One who led *you* out of bondage. "I am *your* God."

Today we live under conditions much like those of the time in which the Ten Commandments were given. We even have many of the same gods. There is Bacchus, the god of wine who is seen everywhere; Vestus, the goddess of the hearth, the provincialism that says *my* land, *my* people, *my* goods, *my* country; Plutus, the god of material things; Diana, Venus, Eros, the gods of sensual pleasure; Mars, the god of war; and Narcissus, who was reflected in the pool. When he saw his image, he began to talk about himself and preen in the reflection. Then, in addition, we tend to make ourselves our gods.

The truth is, though, that whatever claims our ultimate devotion and allegiance is our god. But in effect God says to us, "Thou shall have none of these gods in your life. I must be first in your thought, your life and your work."

Make Him Your Master

In the New Testament, Jesus warns us that "No one can serve two masters" (Matt. 6:24, RSV). But we certainly do try! We do our best to keep all of our allegiances and priorities, and seldom do we ever focus on God and say, "God, thou art sovereign Lord and to Thee I give my best of thought and effort." Instead, by our actions if not our words, we relegate God to last place.

In the first church I served as pastor, a forty-year-old oil engineer called and asked me to have lunch with him. My friend was an interesting man, a brilliant engineer who held several patents in the oil industry. He had just completed a well-organized workshop adjacent to his home, and he wanted me to see it. I was quite impressed with all the machinery, but I was more impressed with his request. "Ernie," he said, "I want you to kneel with me here on the workshop floor and help me give this building, my abilities and all my future achievements to Almighty God." We prayed together and we both were deeply moved. He said afterward that he feared that all he had achieved—his inventions and reputation—had pushed God further down the line of his thoughts and purpose.

My friend's gods had been his talents and his workshop. Our gods may be money, pleasure, wine, or other people—any number of things. But in response to this first commandment, we must choose the Lord our God above everything else so that we are his people and he is our God. Years after these commandments were given to Moses, Joshua picked up on this same theme when he told the Israelites: "Choose you this day whom ye will serve; . . . but as for me and my house, we will serve the LORD" (Josh. 24:15).

QUESTIONS

1. Name one key idea concerning God's priority that you believe is involved in keeping the first commandment.
2. Relate at least one area of your life that would change if God truly held first place in your thoughts and actions.
3. Think through and describe how that change might affect your daily living pattern. Let your imagination explore how radical that change might be.
4. Choose at least one area or goal in which you will make a personal commitment to put God first daily.

. . . .

In order to help you get started in applying this book to your *personal* life, let us use these thought starters as examples for Chapter 2:

1. Recognize an idea. *Believing* in God is not the same as *obeying* him.
2. Relate it specifically in your life. For instance, consider obeying God by "loving your neighbors."
3. Assimilate. Now seek in your daily life to be very sensitive about someone else's needs.
4. Apply. Think and decide on at least one person with some discernible need, and act concretely to meet that need in some practical way.

3

SUBSTITUTE GODS AND POOR EXCUSES

Thou shalt not make unto thee any graven image.

Exodus 20:4

Obedience to God is not simply a matter of putting him first in our lives; God *demands* that we shall make no other gods. When God goes, all the rest of life goes with him. When we substitute something or someone else for him, life becomes a series of poor excuses.

Some years ago, I made a pastoral call on a young mother in the middle of the afternoon. While we spoke, I looked toward the stairway to see a little boy's tousled head peeking through the banister. I tried my best to ignore him, but he kept peeking at me behind his mother's back. Finally the little fellow could restrain himself no longer; he ran halfway down the stairs and called, "Mother, mother, someone has just written all over the wall of my bedroom!" I imagine that mother sees very little humor to this day about the "someone." While a poor excuse is amusing in a child, the same behavior in adults is nothing less than pathetic.

Interlude on a Mountain

The setting in which God gave Moses the Ten Commandments was rugged Mount Sinai in the triangular-shaped Sinai peninsula south of Canaan and east of Egypt. Moses had been up on the mountain for six weeks communing with God. During this time the Israelites were camped on the desert floor at the foot of the mountain. When Moses didn't return as the days went by, the people became restless and decided both Moses and God had deserted them. It was then they asked Aaron to make a god—a golden calf—they could see and worship.

In the meantime God gave Moses the two tablets of stone on which the Ten Commandments were inscribed, and Moses started back down the mountain to where the people were camped. Apparently, Joshua had been waiting for Moses somewhere above the camp, and as the two of them moved closer to the desert floor, they could hear a loud noise. Joshua thought possibly it was the sound of battle, but Moses thought he was hearing sounds of celebration and worship. Then as the two men entered the camp, they saw people dancing around the golden calf that Aaron had made.

At the Foot of the Mountain

While God was giving his commandments to Moses on the mountaintop, the people were breaking them in the valley. Coming down from the mountain in a state of high exultation, Moses stared in disbelief at God's faithless people, and his mood changed as if ice water had been dashed in his face. First his heart froze, then he burned with hot anger at their treachery. In a rage, Moses took the two stone tablets and heaved them to the ground, breaking them into pieces. Then he strode into the midst of the camp and hurled the golden calf into the fire, melting it into fragments which he ground into powder and scattered on the water. The people were then forced to drink the bitter water (Exod. 32:15–20).

Now comes the crux of the drama. Moses turned to Aaron and asked, "How could this thing ever have happened?" Aaron replied the way you and I do when we are caught in a dilemma. He reminded Moses the people were bent on evil and protested that none of this was his fault. Then he went on to say that when the people gave him their gold jewelry, he just threw it in the fire and out came the calf (Exod. 32:21–25).

Let me suggest that Aaron's statement to Moses is just as ludicrous as the little boy's cry to his mother. "Someone (*'someone'*) has just written all over the wall of my bedroom!" Billy, like Aaron, says someone else was responsible. "All I did, Lord, was to throw my energies and talents into competitive living and look what happened—this miserable calf!"

In the Grip of Conviction

Today, we seem very good at making all kinds of excuses. We blame our background, our parents, our society, even our mother-in-law when things go wrong. What we need is to hear again the old Negro spiritual: "It's not my brother, not my sister, but it's *me*, O Lord, standing in the need of prayer." I have said with complete sincerity that if the Word of God never grips me during the week, never convicts me in its judgment and grace, then I have nothing to say to my congregation on Sunday morning.

Moses had been up on the mountain six weeks. Aaron must have been under intense pressure from the people, but notice how he tried to ignore the responsibility for his own leadership and sin. Something was happening to Aaron himself, and he reached the point in his weakness where he wanted most of all to place the fault with someone else.

Aaron was a weak man. Whereas Moses made his excuses before God that he could not speak effectively, Aaron, in this episode, casts aside the personal God, not overtly, but through subterfuge and compromise. Moses earlier had insisted that he could not speak for God, and in response God gave him Aaron as a spokesperson.

At no time do we find Aaron openly defying God. His denial of God is not that simple, and neither is ours. We wouldn't defy God openly—our sin is much more subtle. We simply worship symbols as substitutes for the holy God. Like Aaron, we substitute a symbol—an idol—for God. Perhaps, like Samson, Aaron had compromised so often that "he did not know that the LORD had left him" (Judg. 16:20, RSV).

Yet, for most of us there comes a time, if we have left God out of our lives, when we are confronted with the truth of what happened. It may be in the midnight hour or in a moment of aloneness that the truth dawns on us.

39

The Nightingale and the Peddler

There is the old legend of the nightingale and the peddler. In need of food, the nightingale traded one of his beautiful feathers to the peddler every day for a worm. This went on until the nightingale had lost most of his feathers. One day, aware that he could no longer fly if he lost all his feathers, the nightingale said to the peddler, "I'd like to reverse the process. Let me now trade back to you some of my worms for feathers." But the peddler replied, "Oh, no, you do not understand. I don't trade feathers for worms; I trade only worms for feathers." And the nightingale could no longer fly!

For all of us there comes the day when we have traded too many feathers for worms and the Spirit within us can no longer fly. We no longer feel the joy of being in God's presence. As with Aaron at the foot of Mount Sinai, we then confront the consequence of our sin. Both God's command and the consequences of it if it was not kept were clear. In straightforward language God said:

> You shall not make for yourself a graven image, or any likeness of anything that is in heaven above, or that is in the earth beneath, or that is in the water under the earth; you shall not bow down to them or serve them; for I the LORD your God am a jealous God, visiting the iniquity of the fathers upon the children to the third and fourth generation of those who hate me, but showing steadfast love to thousands of those who love me and keep my commandments (Exod. 20:4–6, RSV).

Substitute Gods and Poor Excuses

I understand these words to mean not so much that God punishes, but that locked into life are absolute consequences that result from our actions. If the Israelites chose God they were shown steadfast love, but if they did not choose God, iniquity visited them to the third and fourth generations. If we leave God out, the results are determined as surely as by the natural laws in the universe.

A Man Chosen of God?

The story of David in the Old Testament is a graphic example of the effect of sin in a man's life, even a man chosen of God. There was a time when the young David, out of a pure heart, could declare, "The Lord is my shepherd, I shall not want;" and "Even though I walk through the valley of the shadow of death, I fear no evil" (Pss. 23:1, 4, RSV). Then one day adulterous poison entered David's heart when he lusted after Bathsheba and plotted her husband's murder by placing him in the front line of battle. He then ordered the men around him to draw back leaving Uriah unprotected. But then when David was confronted by his sin, he repented and poured his heart out to God in Psalm 51:

> Have mercy on me, O God,
>   according to thy steadfast love;
>   according to thy abundant mercy blot out my
>   transgressions.
> Wash me thoroughly from my iniquity,
>   and cleanse me from my sin!

41

For I know my transgressions,
  and my sin is ever before me.
Against thee, thee only, have I sinned,
  and done that which is evil in thy sight,
so that thou art justified in thy sentence
  and blameless in thy judgment.
. . . .
Purge me with hyssop, and I shall be clean;
  wash me, and I shall be whiter than snow.
Fill me with joy and gladness;
  let the bones which thou hast broken rejoice.
Hide thy face from my sins,
  and blot out all my iniquities.

Create in me a clean heart, O God,
  and put a new and right spirit within me.
Cast me not away from thy presence,
  and take not thy holy Spirit from me.
Restore to me the joy of thy salvation,
  and uphold me with a willing spirit
                    (Pss. 51:1–4, 7–12, RSV).

This fact is frequently missed. While David was going on his loose way, leaving God out of his life, his young son, Absalom, was growing up in the home. During that time Absalom's values were being formed, and all of this may well have contributed to his armed revolt against his father in later years. And yet when Joab, David's general, brought David the word of Absalom's death on the battlefield, David, like any father who loves so much it hurts, buried his head in his hands and wept, crying aloud, "Absalom, Absalom, my son, my son!"

Substitute Gods and Poor Excuses

The Closed Door

When people shut the door of their inner lives to God, there begins an insidious process of breakdown in personal integrity, and inevitably that breakdown leads to social chaos. That is exactly what happened to Aaron. His flight from obedience to sin did not happen overnight. It developed by degrees until finally he resorted to a bold-faced lie, telling God in so many words that all he did was throw the gold on the fire. But that wasn't all he did. He actually fashioned the calf with a graving tool; he set up an altar to a substitute god.

Setting Up Substitute Gods

As we view this scene, it is very easy to be self-righteous and judgmental. But we, too, are guilty of setting up our substitute gods. Every time we go through a day and leave out our conversation with God, we are paving the way for building an altar to a false god. By the same token, when we treat God's Word lightly, we are building an altar to a substitute god. But then as we do, it is tragically easy to rationalize our behavior and pollute the air with poor excuses.

From the Bible stories we know the Israelites were a religious people. Always God's most heart-rending problem is with those who know his name, those who should know better. Yes, they were religious; they even named the calf "Jehovah." But the name they gave their god didn't change the reality of their sin. Any time we substitute a god we have thought up or made for the true and living God, we are guilty of breaking this commandment.

It is true that we don't fashion our gods with our hands; we are too sophisticated for that. We are not about to carve a graven image, a molten calf. Instead, we fashion our images with our minds. We love to play around with new isms and theories and are easily impressed with subtle ideas until gradually we begin to create a new image of God for ourselves. But the god we make falls far short of the God Who Is, the God Who Speaks.

It is so important for young people, when they go to college, to examine their accumulated philosophy. Everyone has a philosophy, as our lives always reveal. What we believe in, the god we choose, ultimately shapes and directs our lives.

The contemporary poet W. H. Auden, in his "Christmas Oratorio," puts on the lips of Herod this prayer, pure satire:

> O God, put away justice and truth for we cannot understand them and do not want them. Eternity would bore us dreadfully. Leave Thy heavens and come down to our earth of water clocks and hedges. Become our uncle—look after baby—amuse grandfather—escort Madame to the opera—help Willie with his homework—introduce Muriel to a handsome Naval officer. Be interesting and weak like us, and we will love You as we love ourselves.[2]

Our view of God falls tragically short when compared with God's revelation of himself in Jesus

Christ, in his Word and in his creation.

Dr. J. B. Phillips, in his delightful book, *Your God Is Too Small,* put his finger on our failure to comprehend the awesome greatness of God, for, indeed, our God is much too small. We have fashioned God into our image instead of being fashioned by his.

The Modern Breakdown

The inevitable result of our corrupted ideas about God is seen in the moral breakdown of individual integrity that now infects our society. This is described graphically in Exodus: "And the LORD said to Moses, 'Go down; for your people, whom you brought up out of the land of Egypt, have corrupted themselves; they have turned aside quickly out of the way which I commanded them; they have made for themselves a molten calf, and have worshiped it and sacrificed to it, and said, "These are your gods, O Israel, who brought you up out of the land of Egypt!" ' " (32:7–8, RSV).

When God's standards are abandoned and his laws are defied, we are all adrift and without any sense of purpose and direction. It is for this reason that our study of the Ten Commandments and this one in particular is so important for our spiritual health. It isn't my intention to suggest any kind of blind and rigid legalism, but if we are to avoid being tempted and deceived by the lure of false gods in any form, we must come not only to understand the law but to know the Lawgiver. And it is as we come to know intimately the Lawgiver and Creator of all

45

life that we are not tempted to stray after false gods of any description, and our worship remains true. In the Old and New Testaments, worship is celebration—joy at being in God's presence and in being responsive to his laws and the leading of his Spirit.

It was true, of course, that Aaron's golden calf made no demands on the people. That's the way it is with our false gods. When we shape them with our minds and control them with our philosophy or theology, they make no demands on us. However, neither Aaron's calf nor any of our false gods can *guide* or *forgive* us. Only the God of Israel—your God and mine as revealed in Jesus Christ—can forgive sin and guide us into a lifestyle of wholeness, self-acceptance and joy.

When God Is Missing

Unfortunately, though, I encountered a symbol of our times when I visited the Prayer Room at the United Nations building in New York. This sterile prayer room contained no symbols of worship—no cross, no Star of David. The only furnishings were a row of captain's chairs around the room and a potted plant. There was nothing to offend anyone and nothing to inspire. I found no God there who called me to obedience, who loved me, who would guide me.

But God, in Jesus Christ, has shown us the fallacy of chasing after gods of our own invention—silent, impersonal gods that demand nothing from us and show no feeling toward us. There was nothing vague or abstract about Jesus. As he walked the hot and dusty roads of first-century Palestine, Jesus showed us what God is like. God actually walked among us, for, as John wrote, "the law was given by Moses, *but* grace and truth came by Jesus Christ. No man hath seen God at any time; the only begotten Son, which is in the bosom of the Father, he hath declared *him*" (John 1:17–18). God, for the first time, walked in human form among people and "we beheld his glory."

Not Definition but Devotion

Our hope, in keeping the law of God, is to walk in fellowship with Jesus Christ. God doesn't require definition so much as he desires devotion and obedience. And there is a vast difference between being intellectually correct, and being obedient to God. He walked among us so that we would know him. And in knowing him, God would become our top priority. We would have no other God but him.

The good news in this world, where the loss of personal integrity and faith has resulted in a chaotic society, is that Jesus Christ is Lord. This is our message and mission. We are not called to defend him, but to love him. He is our hope.

When Aaron was questioned about the golden calf, he could stand right in front of it and lie, making excuses, but he couldn't have lied in the presence of a holy God on a mountain. Saul of Tarsus could assault and imprison early Christians in obedience to Jewish laws, but when he met Jesus, he fell on his knees—and hate and murder left him forever.

God in Jesus Christ comes to us again and again. He says to every modern Aaron who is making excuses, "I am come that they might have life, and that they might have *it* more abundantly" (John 10:10). He instructs us to "love the Lord thy God with all thy heart, and with all thy soul, and with all thy mind. . . . [and] thy neighbour as thyself" (Matt. 22:37, 39). And he informs us that "by this shall all *men* know that ye are my disciples, if ye have love one to another" (John 13:35).

When God becomes that real to us, he will be first—we will need no other gods—and we will no longer need poor excuses, for the poor substitutes will be replaced by the Savior.

Questions

1. What is the one way you effectively "silence" God in your life?
2. Other than necessary family and work obligations, what areas of your life now receive the highest percentage of your energy, time and money?
3. In this chapter, it is noted that we are likely to shape idols with our minds rather than with our hands. Name at least one "mind-shaped graven image" you have made as a substitute for God.
4. How do you plan to "destroy" your substitute god and worship the true God faithfully?

4

PROFANITY WITHOUT WORDS

Thou shalt not take the name of the LORD thy God in vain; for the LORD will not hold him guiltless that taketh his name in vain.

Exodus 20:7

Not every one that saith unto me, Lord, Lord, shall enter into the kingdom of heaven; but he that doeth the will of my Father which is in heaven.

Matthew 7:21

The commandment that has been understood the least perhaps is the one concerning God's name—the commandment concerning profanity. Usually we quibble about this with the question of the words we use, words that have to include God's name to be breaking the commandment. In fact, this commandment really hits at the heart of our whole life. It directs itself to the gap that exists between our *profession* and our *performance*. The profanity to which it refers has little to do with our words except as they relate to our *actions*.

The Importance of Names

Names were very important in the times when the Bible was written. For example, "Samu-el" was the name given to a son whose parents waited a long, long time for him. When the child was born, they named him Samuel, meaning "asked of God." Actually, whenever you find *el* in the Bible, it refers to God—Ezeki-*el,* Isra-*el* and so on. After crafty and wily Jacob had confronted God through an entire night, he was renamed Israel—"wrestler with God." Other names were of special significance in the

Bible. Isaac was an important name. When Sarah first heard the promise of God that she and Abraham would have a child, the Bible says she laughed in derision. But God's promise was kept, and Isaac was born. Abraham and Sarah, old in years, were so thrilled with that new little life that they named their son Isaac, which meant "laughter-in-joy."

A census taker came to the door, probably bored with the routine at the end of the day. With paper in hand, he asked the woman who answered the door, "How many children live here?" "Well, let's see," she replied, "there's Horace and Muriel and Sarah." The census taker stopped her. "Lady, I didn't ask you for their names, I asked you for the number."

"My children don't have numbers, they have names," she responded impatiently.

In this computer age, we all have felt that lady's exasperation. I'm always frustrated when I receive a computer letter. I want to shout, "I'm not number 46719264. I have a name. Treat me like a person."

God Has a Name

We need to look at this with that in mind. It is crisp and clear. "Thou shalt not take the *name* of the LORD thy God in vain; for the LORD will not hold him guiltless that taketh his *name* in vain." We are not to use it carelessly. God has a *name!* His name is Jehovah! He is not an it. He is not computerized. He is not a great "someone," somewhere. Behind the name of God stands a Being and a Personality. The Hebrews recognized this.

In the early days of Israel there were those who swore "by Jehovah," which I suppose is like our saying, "cross my heart and hope to die." In effect, they were saying, "By Jehovah, I will do this," but then they didn't. They were using God's name in vain because they said they would do something, but they simply did not. They didn't mean it.

When I was in seminary, one of my classmates had a brother who was the captain of the football team at a college in California. This young man had taken the name of Jesus Christ as his own, and vowed that he was his disciple. His life, however, began to be anything but disciplined. He lived a sinful and reckless life—a disgrace to the name he professed to carry. My friend wrote to his brother and said, "Brother, you do one of two things;—either straighten up your life or drop the name of Christ. But don't carry his name and live the way you are."

This letter convicted the young man of his sin, and he wrote back, thanking his brother for loving him enough to write as he had. Happily, both men are now ordained ministers and both are faithful to the name they carry and the gospel they preach in the name of Jesus Christ.

What does it mean to carry the name of Jesus Christ in our day? Does it make any difference in our style of life? Does it make a difference to the businessman? In the way we figure our income taxes?

The Meaning of Profanity

In this third commandment, God is really talking about the difference between our words and our performance. *Profanity is denying him with our lives while we profess him with our speech.*

Actually, the word *profanity* comes from two Latin roots, *pro,* which means before, and *fane,* which means temple. In its original use profanity, then, refers to the holy place—"before the temple"—the misuse or desecration of that place.

Today, when the sense of holiness is squeezed out and there are no holy places, we are in danger of living our lives in profanity, and our words are a reflection of that. In the deepest sense, this commandment addresses our lives as well as our words. Our profanity, if we use God's name carelessly in taking oaths or in swearing, is really a clue. If we go through life swearing in God's name, it's a clue that God really doesn't mean much to us at all. We cannot feel the reality of his presence and the sense of awe it brings while using his name carelessly or irreverently.

There are people who wouldn't think of saying "damn" but who break this commandment all the time by their gossip and their misuse of persons. They profane the very being of God. The prophet Jeremiah had some strong things to say on this subject:

> Stand in the gate of the LORD's house, and proclaim there this word, and say, Hear the word of the LORD, all you men of Judah who enter these gates to worship the LORD. Thus says the LORD of hosts, the God of Israel, Amend your ways and your doings, and I will let you dwell in this place. Do not trust in these deceptive words: "This is the temple of the LORD,

the temple of the LORD, the temple of the LORD" (Jer. 7:2–4, RSV).

Again and again, God says through the prophets, "Who requires of you this tramping of my courts?" (Isa. 1:12, RSV). What he means is, "I'm tired of your coming to church and going through all the religious motions, and yet your lives are lived as if I didn't even exist." He is saying, "You have all the words. You chant, 'The temple of the Lord, the temple of the Lord,' but it doesn't make any difference what you say with your mouth if your life doesn't back it up." In other words, if life doesn't match the words, that is profanity.

But then Jeremiah went on to say:

> For if you truly amend your ways and your doings, if you truly execute justice one with another, if you do not oppress the alien, the fatherless or the widow, or shed innocent blood in this place, and if you do not go after other gods to your own hurt, then I will let you dwell in this place, in the land that I gave of old to your fathers for ever.

> Behold, you trust in deceptive words to no avail. Will you steal, murder, commit adultery, swear falsely, burn incense to Baal, and go after other gods that you have not known, and then come and stand before me in this house, which is called *by my name*, and say "We are delivered!"—only to go on doing all these abominations? Has this house, which is called *by my name*, become a den of robbers in your eyes? Behold, I myself have seen it, says the LORD. Go now to my place that was in Shiloh, where I

made *my name* dwell at first, and see what I did
to it for the wickedness of my people Israel. And
now, because you have done all these things, says
the LORD, and when I spoke to you persistently you
did not listen, and when I called you, you did not
answer, therefore I will do to the house which is
called *by my name,* and in which you trust, and to
the place which I gave to you and to your fathers,
as I did to Shiloh. And I will cast you out of my
sight, as I cast out all your kinsmen, all the offspring
of Ephraim (7:5–15, RSV, Italics mine).

I have come to appreciate that sometimes what
we call swearing may not be swearing at all in the
deepest sense of the word. I think God wants us to
care deeply for the kinds of hurts that are destroying
people in this modern-day world. Our problem is
that our anger, like our expletives, is most often because *we* have been offended and not because we
are offended at all the evil and apathy around us
that is blaspheming God's name.

Anguish and Anger

To be centered in oneself, in one's own little world
and ego, may create another form of idolatry, but
feeling the anguish and the anger can be purifying
if it flows from the love of God and focuses on compassion for the world and then results in *action.*

Jesus picked up on this theme in the closing words
of the Sermon on the Mount when he said that anyone who heard his words and put them into practice
would be like a person who builds on a solid foun-

dation. The winds will blow and shriek, and that house will stand. But anyone who keeps hearing his words and does not put them into practice will be like a person who builds on shifting sand. When the winds and the rains come, the house will fall (Matt. 7:24–37).

God gave us these commandments so that we might focus on him first—on his being—and then that we would be true and honest in our living. We have heard these words from the New Testament: "Better to say *yes* and *no*, and stop this nonsense about all the vows when you don't intend to keep them, for that is profanity."

In the book of Genesis we have the story of two interesting and complex men—Jacob and Esau. Theirs was the struggle between the sensate and the spiritual world. Jacob was a rascal. Wily and crafty, he was a cheater as a young man, but he met his match in his Uncle Laban. Jacob had fallen in love with his cousin Rachel and agreed to work seven years for her hand in marriage. But when it came time for the marriage, Laban cheated Jacob by substituting a heavily veiled Leah, Rachel's older sister. Too late, he realized he had the wrong girl. And so, by agreement, Jacob worked seven more years for Rachel. But the "Cheating Uncle Laban" was in turn cheated by Jacob. When Jacob left, fourteen years after he started working for Laban, he took not only his two wives, Leah and Rachel, but also the best of his uncle's flocks. And he also carried off the family jewels and the silver.

Profanity without Words

While Jacob was a wily man, his brother Esau was earthy. He was a hunter and fisherman—"a man's man." Esau arrived home one day after a long hunting expedition, ravenously hungry. Wily Jacob, knowing that Esau had been gone for several days, mixed up an aromatic pot of stew. It smelled delicious. When Esau smelled the stew, he asked his brother to share it with him. But Jacob said, "Whoa, brother. I've got a deal I'd like to make with you. You know that birthright Dad told us about? Tell you what I'll do. I'll trade you. You give me that birthright and you can have this whole pot of stew." Esau didn't even blink! He said, "Great!" and sat down to eat. He filled himself full.

Even though Jacob was confused and deceitful, he still had an inner yearning for the spiritual implications of God's blessing through the birthright. Jacob apparently had at least a little sensitivity to God's promise to Abraham that from their family would come a great nation and the future Messiah. There was a glimmer of hope for Jacob, but Esau could care less. He traded the stew for the birthright and satisfied his hunger pangs but sacrificed his future. The Bible calls Esau "a profane man."

Losing a Sense of Wonder

The temptations of the Esau-syndrome plague us today. On the one hand, we feel a sense of hopelessness with the threats of crime, terrorism and war. On the other hand, we are desensitized by the scien-

59

tific wonders of computers, space travel, laser technology and medical "miracles." All of this can be a threat to our sense of God's presence. The noise and dazzle of today's society can so easily drown out the "still, small voice." We are in danger of losing our awareness of God and his transcendence. G. K. Chesterton, the late British author, remarked some years ago as he stood in Times Square, New York, with all its blinking, colored lights: "Wouldn't it be a shame if we lived in a world full of wonders and lost the ability to feel the sense of wonder?"

In Peter Berger's book, *Rumor of Angels,* he speaks of that loss of transcendence in our generation and writes,

> We are, whether we like it or not, in a situation in which transcendence has been reduced to a rumor. A rediscovery of the supernatural will be above all a regaining of openness in our perception of reality. The principal moral benefit of religion is that it permits a confrontation with the age in which one lives in a perspective that transcends the age and puts it in proportion.[3]

When God's holy being is honored with a sense of reverence and awe, and we recognize the disparity between our performance and our vows, then we are open, wide open, to fulfilling his love with one another. But when God is gone, we are in danger. Our profanity, in words and careless speech, is again but a clue, a symptom of a much deeper problem. Our words are not so important in themselves, but, like headaches, they are clues to something deeper.

God says, "When you can begin to use my name so carelessly, it means you really don't have the appropriate sense of awe and of love for me."

Jesus Is a Friend of Mine

Another of my seminary classmates had been a construction engineer before coming to school. He told me that he had been working on a building in Oklahoma when a truck driver backed up and ran the rear wheels right over the concrete forms the men were working on. In his anger, my friend had unleashed a profane tirade that was a scorcher. The truck door opened and out came a man six and one-half-feet tall. He walked up to Joe, a very short man, who thought for a moment he was going to be squashed. Instead, the big man said, "I'm sorry I broke your forms. I'll come back and fix them on my own time. But I want you to know that you've taken the name of a very good friend of mine in vain and his name is Jesus Christ." He climbed back in his truck and drove off. Joe said, "I just stood there shaking. He was a bigger man than I was, by more than the breadth of his shoulders." Joe said that this encounter over the profanity of God's name eventually led him to Christ and to seminary.

Woodrow Wilson, president of the United States and architect of the League of Nations, was the son of a Presbyterian minister. He told the story of how one day, in his father's presence, a man, rough of disposition and character, swore, using God's name in vain. Then realizing that the minister was there, he paused and said, "Oh, I'm sorry, sir, for offending you." Woodrow Wilson's father looked at him and said, "You haven't offended *me,* but you have offended *God!*"

Long after giving this commandment to Moses on Sinai, God once again emphasized the importance of his name through the prophet Isaiah:

> For to us a child is born,
>   to us a son is given;
> and the government will be upon his shoulder,
>   and *his name* will be called
> "Wonderful Counselor, Mighty God,
> Everlasting Father, Prince of Peace."
> Of the increase of his government and of peace
>   there will be no end (Isa. 9:6–7, RSV, italics mine).

And again Isaiah writes:

> Behold, a young woman shall conceive and bear a son, and shall call *his name* Immanu-el (7:14, RSV, italics mine).

God with Us

Matthew repeats that prophecy and then adds the important words, "which being interpreted is, God with us." Matthew also makes it clear that this "son," who will be called Jesus, will be the new name when Immanuel comes to redeem his people. Matthew then adds, "And thou shalt call his *name* JESUS: for he shall save his people from their sins" (Matt. 1:21, italics mine).

Profanity without Words

We are no longer confronted just with the law, but with the Lawgiver, with God. We recognize that it is not just a broken law with which we must deal, but a broken love. But we have a new chance. The "Wonderful Counselor," "Mighty God," "Everlasting Father," "Prince of Peace," is incarnate in Jesus Christ.

When Jesus taught his disciples to pray, "Our Father, Who art in Heaven, *hallowed be Thy name,*" he was saying that we are not to use the Father's name carelessly. This, I believe, is an echo of the third commandment God gave Moses on the mountain—neither with our lips nor with our lives shall we take the name of Almighty God in vain. This commandment says, match your performance with your profession as long as you bear the name of Christ.

Questions

1. In your experience, what do you think is the most common way people break this commandment today?
2. Relate "taking God's name in vain" to some experience or characteristic behavior in your life.
3. If you were to take more seriously the holiness of God—his being and his name—describe some ways you would expect your life to change.
4. Describe at least one way that you plan to change to make the commandment mean more to you in your daily life.

5

SUNDAY AND THE MODERN DILEMMA

Remember the sabbath day, to keep it holy. Six days shalt thou labour, and do all thy work: But the seventh day is the sabbath of the LORD thy God: in it thou shalt not do any work, thou, nor thy son, nor thy daughter, thy manservant, nor thy maidservant, nor thy cattle, nor thy stranger that is within thy gates: For in six days the Lord made heaven and earth, the sea, and all that in them is, and rested the seventh day: wherefore the LORD blessed the sabbath day, and hallowed it.

Exodus 20:8–11

This commandment concerning the sabbath is addressed to the whole human family, and the principle behind it, of course, is the setting aside of a proportionate time in which to focus one's mind and energy on God.

In Ezekiel, God says, "Wherefore I caused them to go forth out of the land of Egypt, and brought them into the wilderness. And I gave them my statutes, and shewed them my judgments, which *if* a man do, he shall even live in them. Moreover also I gave them my sabbaths, to be a sign between me and them, that they might know that I *am* the LORD that sanctify them" (20:10–12). The word *sanctify* means "to set apart." In other words, God wants us to set apart the sabbath day as a time of worship and praise.

Of Worship and Work

Among all of God's creation, we alone can stand in awe of God's sunrises and sunsets. To us has been given the capacity to enjoy the awesome beauty of all that God has made. But contemplation, meditation and even relaxation require the resolve to use one's energies for those purposes and then the exercise of will to *do* it. Both our worship and our work are expressions of our energy and our wills.

God knows we need *rest for our bodies* and *stimulation for our souls,* so he gave us this law to protect us from our foolishness and to surprise us with its benefit. The sensitive soul begins to hunger for God's presence in praise. The Psalms are full of the songs of praise to the glory of God and the maturation of the soul. While worship in some liturgical form of word and sacrament has always been at the center of sabbath keeping, at least part of our time needs to be spent in the joyful rejuvenation that comes from contemplating God's creation. One beautiful hymn puts it thoughtfully:

> This is my Father's world,
>   and to my listening ears,
> All nature sings, and round me rings
>   the music of the spheres,
> This is my Father's world:
>   I rest me in the thought.
> Of rocks and trees, of skies and seas;
>   His hand the wonders wrought.
>
> This is my Father's world,
>   the birds their carols raise,
> The morning light, the lily white,
>   declare their maker's praise.
> This is my Father's world;
>   He shines in all that's fair;
> In the rustling grass I hear Him pass,
>   He speaks to me everywhere.[4]

From the very beginning, God has called his people to stop, contemplate him and rest in his love and forgiveness. In Genesis 2:1–3, after God had created Adam and Eve on the sixth day, he rested on the seventh day. When God spoke the words of the Ten Commandments to Moses, he said, "Remember the sabbath day, to keep it holy. . . . For *in* six days the Lord made heaven and earth, the sea, and all that in them *is,* and rested the seventh day; wherefore, the LORD blessed the sabbath day, and hallowed it."

An Ancient Commandment for Modern Man

When this commandment was given to Moses, life was rural and agricultural. There were no power mowers or power boats or snowmobiles from Dan to Beersheba. In the midst of our modern noise and activity, and hectic, frantic fun, how can we understand and apply this ancient commandment to our own times?

Herman Wouk, the well-known Jewish author, was met one day by a harried theatrical producer who said to him, "I do not covet your religion but I covet your sabbath."

How many people are there who wish they could be really quiet—unhurried, unharried, with time for reflection and meditation? Our day is so complex! Even while we worship in our sanctuaries, someone has to run the electric dynamos that provide power for lights. Someone has to provide heat. There are police forces protecting our persons; firemen, physicians, surgeons, nurses and many other people who contribute to our welfare twenty-four hours a day, every day. Our culture could not survive if these services were not provided every moment.

It seems to me that it is extremely difficult for us to observe the sabbath for two reasons: (1) We live in a pluralistic society, with a variety of religious views and convictions, or no religious views at all, and (2) our high-speed, complex, industrial age seems to require work around the clock, seven days a week, three hundred and sixty-five days a year.

Which Day?

There are other problems with the observance of the sabbath. One of the earliest problems was which day shall we keep? When the law was given, there was no question about it. "Sabbath" for the Jew meant from sundown Friday to sundown Saturday. In the Christian church, the resurrection of Jesus Christ occurred on the first day of the week, as did Pentecost. So the early church named the first day of the week, "The Lord's Day," and Sunday became the sabbath for Christians.

From the giving of this commandment to Moses on Mount Sinai down to the present time, rules of sabbath behavior have been laid out and debated. The principle behind the sabbath is not so much the day as it is the thought and the appropriate *activity*. Throughout the ages such a day has been fought for.

Charlemagne, in 787, passed a law in the ancient empire for sabbath observance. King Henry III, in 1239, passed a law in England for sabbath observance. Our forefathers, the founders of the colony in Virginia in 1610, passed a law for sabbath observance. If you grew up on the east coast, you know that many states have "blue laws" in their efforts to preserve the sabbath.

Where there are state laws or local laws or "blue laws" defending the sabbath, they are precisely on moral grounds. It is the same kind of logic that is involved in "thou shalt not murder." This happens to be one of the commandments—"Thou shalt not kill"—but it is also part of our civil code. It is not for *religious* reasons, but for moral reasons (or what the state or government determines is best for the well-being of its people) that these laws exist. Thus, even the secular person has to wrestle with the question of the sabbath, a time in which a person does not *have* to work but when we may exercise our thoughts and energies in a whole new direction.

A Different Kind of Desert

The sabbath was given to the Israelites in the wilderness. It came at a time when they were wandering in the desert. It may well be that we, too, are in a different kind of desert as we struggle with the complexity of demands made upon us today. A right understanding of God's law and his reasons for it can be as refreshing for the soul of modern man as it was for the Israelites. They, in their preoccupation with the work of their hands and because of the surrounding bleakness of the territory, were in danger of losing God's reality. So are we.

It is important for us to establish the fact that God gave us this law as he did the others because he loves us. If we could but establish this as part of our understanding of God's law, we would be halfway home. God did not give the law because he was punitive or mean, or wanted to spoil our fun. He gave us the law that we might find order and meaning and design and purpose—*fulfillment*—in this created order that he fashioned.

The Christian must turn to the New Testament for a deeper understanding of what this commandment means. On a typical day in the life of Jesus (Mark 2:27–28) he was hounded by his critics. Legalists, who could quote the Scripture, had the law all figured out. They hounded Jesus for healing people on the sabbath day. They hounded him because they said his disciples worked on the sabbath when they picked some corn, ground it off in their hands and began to munch on it. They ate raw corn.

In Jesus' time more than fifteen hundred laws had been devised by the Pharisees and Scribes, thirty-nine of which dealt precisely with work. But one of these laws was really important, "Thou shalt not thresh or winnow or reap or prepare a meal on the sabbath." The disciples managed to fracture all four of these basic laws in one fell swoop on the day the authorities accused them of working. By tearing the ear off the corn shock, they reaped; by shucking it, they were winnowing and threshing; and in doing all of this, they were preparing a meal in their hands.

A Burden or a Blessing

As further proof as to just how silly things had become, the Jewish religious authorities said that the carrying of any kind of a "burden" was work. For example, if a ribbon was pinned on your dress, you were carrying a burden, but if it were sewn on your dress, it became part of the fabric and wasn't a burden. By that kind of logic, we can assume that wearing false teeth would be carrying a burden!

Mark's story of the episode in the cornfield was followed immediately by another incident in which Jesus challenged the absurdity of the sabbath laws. It was in the synagogue and on the sabbath that Jesus healed a man with a withered hand. Then, with eyes flashing, he looked at the Pharisees and scribes and said, "Is it lawful to do good on the sabbath days, or to do evil? to save life, or to kill?" (Mark 3:4). It was then that Jesus spelled out clearly and crisply the principles that apply to us today. He said, "The sabbath was made for man, and not man for the sabbath" (Mark 2:27). How profound that is! God did not establish the law to crush us. He gave us the law to defend us from our own foolishness and free us to live as children of God.

At another time and in another place, Jesus had said, "Neither is new wine put into old wineskins; if it is, the skins burst, and the wine is spilled, and the skins are destroyed; but new wine is put into fresh wineskins, and so both are preserved" (Matt. 9:17, RSV). Jesus came to establish a new fellowship, a new society, and give us a completely new frame of reference for all of life. And this life was freedom and joy—not a slavery to nit-picking rules.

Our forefathers seemed to have missed this. The sabbath became grim. Many of us can remember when, in our childhood, many families would not buy a newspaper or turn on a radio. No meals were prepared. Everything had to be done the day before. One man said he couldn't wait until Sunday was over because it was six whole days until another one came along. There was nothing to do! God didn't intend this to be a day when we are glum. This attitude was just the opposite to what Jesus had to say. He meant the sabbath to be a time when we are refreshed in mind and spirit.

Our Need for Rest and Reflection

We need a work/rest cycle. We are so fashioned by God that we need something to do. And if we don't have tasks that keep us busy and give us a sense of purpose, we become restless or depressed. But at the same time we need rest and relaxation. We need time to reflect and time to worship. To violate this basic law of God is to jeopardize our physical well-being. We become overanxious and compulsive.

The Psalmist tells us that we are wonderfully made. And we are. While our physical bodies require rest to be rejuvenated with energy, our spiritual lives are renewed by action and involvement. To find spiritual refreshment, we must engage our minds and wills in some creative way. If we leave bread out of our diet, the body begins to crave it. Ironically, if we leave God out of our lives, we want him less and less. But, as we put God into our lives in a creative way, we will want him more and more.

Our sovereign loving God has said in effect, "You must set aside part of your goods and your time." He suggested one-tenth of our goods and one-seventh of our time. For physical and spiritual reasons, there must be order and balance in our lives. So, God gives us the law because he knows how irresponsible we are going to be about ourselves and about our relationship to him, to others and even to ourselves.

And God's laws are something we can always count on. When we look at a tree, stark in the midst of winter, it takes faith to see that the tree will have green buds in the months to follow, and then beautiful leaves. God gives us the tides of the ocean. For some, it is restful just to sit by the seashore and watch the tides ebb and flow. We know without doubt when we walk in low tide along the seashore, that in due course, it will be high tide. Similarly, the seasons come and go.

Free to Choose

A tree can't make a decision. God decided for it. The tree has a time of reproduction and a time of rest. The circles in its trunk tell when those times occurred. A tree can't decide, but a person can decide. God made us free people, to choose, to be wise enough to set aside some time and devote ourselves in thought and action and life to the refreshment of body and spirit.

The same certainty of rhythm regulates our own physical and spiritual life. The important thing is for us to go in God's flow—rest for the physical activity and worship for the spiritual.

From time to time, someone will say to me, "I can worship God easier in the out-of-doors than I can in church." To be sure a person can worship God in the out-of-doors. There is much we can learn about God in the wonders of nature. But we can never learn the nature of God from nature. For balance, a person needs both work and worship, play and rest. We also need time for covenant worship with others. Enjoying the out-of-doors with the family can be a great and refreshing experience on the sabbath day. But the praise of God in his creation can never be a substitute for the exercise of mind and heart in praise in the fellowship of his people.

You've probably never bothered to count, but a person twenty-one years of age has had three years of sabbaths in his lifetime. At age thirty-five, we have had five years of Sundays. And by age seventy, we have experienced ten years of Sundays—ten years of Sundays in which to develop a spiritual life. God anticipated our needs long before we had them, and he gave us this law of the sabbath because he loves us and wants us to know and understand him better. He wants us to be enriched and to enjoy life to the fullest by following his design and being in step with his rhythm for us.

Oh, the wonder of it all is that this great God, in his love for us, created a universe where we alone can say "thank you" and can discern.

It is an intriguing, exciting thought to realize, with all the color and the beauty to be seen in our day, how full and rich life can be. If we find the balance between engagement by work and all of the joy it brings, and the time of rest and quiet, of unhurried contemplation of God's being—his worship, his world, his work and his will—then we will discover how to be whole persons. We will know that this law is a law of love. By keeping the sabbath holy, we keep ourselves whole.

Questions

1. Choose either of the following to discuss:
   a. What would you consider necessary in the keeping of this commandment today?
   b. What would you include as breaking this commandment today?
2. Describe ways in which you yourself typically keep this commandment. How do you break it?
3. In order to keep this commandment more obediently, what do you need to change in your living pattern?
4. Choose one thing you will change and describe what benefit you think it might bring you.

6

YOUR FAMILY
AND YOUR FAITH

Honour thy father and thy mother.

Exodus 20:12

Notice the *position* of the fifth commandment. It is crucial in God's great design for order on the earth. God sets us within the family in order that through its support system of love we may be able to step out and relate to other persons in the world. We need emotional and spiritual stability. If our family home does not provide that, then the church, the extended family of Jesus Christ, may well do so.

The family is the cornerstone of civilization, and at the base of the family is respect for parents. Therefore, the basis of our society is the respect and honor we give our parents.

"Honour thy father and thy mother." The Greek word for honor is *tim-a-o,* which means to "place a value on." God has always placed great value on fathers and mothers.

The Meaning of Headship

The father's headship in the ancient world was undisputed. He had the power of life and death, as in the story of Abraham and Isaac in Genesis 22, and Jephthah's sacrifice of his daughter in Judges

11. According to Exodus 21:7, the father even had the right to sell his daughter as a bondservant. But the other side of the coin is the protection and security the father provided. Fathers constituted the "elders," those who ruled over the clans and tribes of Israel. They were to be "wise, understanding, and experienced men, according to your tribes, and I will appoint them as your heads" (Deut. 1:13, RSV). They were the decision makers.

In Jesus' time, mothers were looked upon with great esteem. As a twelve-year-old boy in the temple, Jesus told his mother that he had to be in his father's house. And we read that his mother "treasured all these things in her heart."

Luke gives us the story of a woman grieving over her dead son: "And when the Lord saw her, he had compassion on her, and said unto her, Weep not" (Luke 7:13). Luke goes on to tell us that when Jesus touched the coffin, the man was restored to life. Women traveled with Jesus, as we read in Luke 8, and gave him support out of their private means. When Jesus hung from the cross, he recognized his mother standing there, and said, "Woman, behold your son!" Then, he told the disciple whom he loved to care for her. Truly, Jesus Christ honored his mother.

The Christian tradition has always honored older people, also. In primitive societies, older people were often left on their own to wander away from the tribe and die. In some cultures, older people were ordered out when they were not productive any longer. Our heritage, however, has preserved the emphasis on tender concern for those older in years. In fact, many scholars believe the commandment to honor thy father and thy mother is addressed to adults, not children, because so much has been written elsewhere concerning respect for parents by children.

An Interlocking Relationship

In the New Testament, we find the apostle Paul has set this commandment in a broader context to include not just parent and child, but parent to parent, husbands to wives, parents to children and children to parents. The emphasis is upon an interlocking relationship that exists within the family unit. How vitally important this is in our time!

To the Ephesians, Paul wrote some very personal thoughts, "Wives, be subject to your husbands." I have had women say to me before their weddings, "I don't want anything like that in the wedding ceremony!" But nothing here can be taken out of its context of total accountability in the family, "as to the Lord." "Be subject to your husbands as to the Lord." Following quickly, we read, "Husbands, love your wives, as Christ loved the church and gave himself up for her." If husbands really loved like that, then Christian wives would have no problem being "subject" to their husbands. There is an inner accountability to one another "as to the Lord" that translates "be subject" out of a demeaning or subordinate role right into compatability where the father and mother make one whole (Eph. 5:22–23).

There is a family interdependence and the key phrase is this: "Be subject *to one another*, out of *reverence for Christ*" (Eph. 5:21, RSV). That is the groundwork for a family, and how real that becomes is determined by how real we are with one another. Our Lord's forgiveness of us is important. It is his forgiveness that can free a parent. Whatever the age of the parent or the child, when something goes wrong, don't hesitate to say, "I'm sorry." And pray to really mean it. That is not demeaning for parents, it is freeing. It teaches children what the love and forgiveness of God is all about. Personal relationships can begin to focus when parents acknowledge their failures to themselves, to each child and to God.

The Prayer of a Young Mother

A young mother prayed, "They are asleep, O God, and I am tired. Make me all I want them to be; strong, true and great artists. Let me mend their souls as well as tend to their bodies. Help me to learn the secret of trust in thee from their trust in me."

In the rural and agricultural economy of Bible times, families were drawn together by many forces that no longer exist as they once did. Families did many chores together and they were interdependent for food, clothing, transportation and a dozen other things. But the modern family's schedule finds the father commuting and spending much less time with

83

his family than his father and grandfather did.

We often romanticize the role of mothers. This can leave many with a feeling of guilt or failure in the parenting process. But look at the picture some unknown poet has drawn:

Every Home an Altar

If every home were an altar,
　Where hearts weighed down with care
Could find sustaining strength and grace
　In sweet uplift of prayer.

Then solved would be earth's problems,
　Banished sin's curse and blight;
For God's own love would radiate
　From every altar light.

Today many mothers have discovered ways to express their gifts of service and education and still maintain a quality relationship with their families. Many mothers would feel fulfilled if they could find avenues of communication and talent in addition to their home. For all mothers, Elton Trueblood's words in his book, *Your Other Vocation,* could be helpful. He writes:

If a woman can come to see her work in the guidance of a home as a ministry, a way in which she can fulfill the intention of God for her, she may be able to glorify her life in her own eyes, and that is what is needed first. Motherhood is not merely a biological phenomena; it is not merely dull domestic work; it is not merely a job. It is a holy calling. Behold, your calling is the heartening admonition to the tired

mother who envies her husband his interesting public
work, as it is to the factory worker who envies the
lot of the white collar worker.[5]

Paul has an important word for fathers as well
as children when he says, "Children, obey your parents in everything, for this pleases the Lord. Fathers,
do not provoke your children, lest they become discouraged" (Col. 3:20–21, RSV). If a father enters into
a relationship with his children only at the point of
punishment, he is likely to do it with irritation. There
is a little cartoon of the boy who comes to his father
with his school grades. Obviously, from the father's
expression, they are less than acceptable. Father is
scowling and about to blast the child when the little
fellow says, "Dad, which do you suppose it is, heredity or environment?"

Mutual Responsibility

But the environment that promotes reverence and
respect for parents is a mutual responsibility. A father must assume his rightful place of leadership and
decision making, not just be a provider of material
things. At times, fathers may excuse their lack of
family involvement with the excuse, "Look at all I'm
providing for my family!" I find that most of the time
wife and children agree: "We'll take less of the fringe
benefits if we can have more of *him*."

As parents, though, we teach our children not by
what we say so much as by what we are and do.
Even within a rather harsh family climate, if there

is a deep love, the children are able to sift and sort. They feel more threatened by inconsistencies and contradictions.

In his *Fairy Tales,* Grimm tells the story of the home where the father had come to live with the family. The daughter-in-law deeply resented this. The situation was grim; the air was tense. One day the old man was at the table, eating noisily. Finally, the daughter-in-law, in irritation, said, "If you're going to eat like a pig, you can eat in the corner," and she sat him a place in the corner. Then one day, as his old hands were shaking, he dropped his earthen bowl and it broke. The daughter-in-law said, "If you're going to eat like a pig and act like a pig, we'll make a trough for you and you can eat out of that." And they did. Later, the son of the old father noticed his little four-year-old boy, the apple of his eye, playing with some bits of wood. "Son, what are you doing?" he asked. The boy, looking for parental approval said, "I'm making a trough so some day I can feed my own father and mother."

A wise person has observed that up to age twelve or so a child does what a parent says. After that, a child does what a parent *does.* Kindness, love and respect for one another is communicated to our children every day by our words and actions. Every time a parent says to the other, "I love you," a child gets a head start in living a fulfilling life.

A mother told her daughter to do something, and the girl replied, "I don't want to do that. Why *should* I?" The mother replied, "Because your mother said so." The girl then asked, "Well, why should that make it right?" And the mother replied, "I guess it's because *her* mother told her, and her mother's mother told her and so on." With that the daughter put her hands on her hips and said, "I wonder whoever started *that* silly custom." If she had been a little wiser, she would have known that God started this "silly custom."

Home Is Where It All Begins

Looking at the sequence of the commandments, we find that God gave us a sense of authority and responsibility within the home that there might be order and security in society. If a child does not learn respect for authority at home, he or she is not likely to learn it anywhere else. A great deal of the brokenness and belligerent behavior of the present generation comes about because parents were not able or willing to exercise proper parental authority within the home. The children dominated the parents, and the parents were obedient to the children! Some parents are even intimidated by their children and are hesitant to enforce consistent boundaries. They do not enforce accountability for behavior because they are not secure in their children's love and are fearful of "not being liked by their offspring." How tragic!

A mother was talking to her two little children one day as they visited Grandpa's farm. The occasion brought back a flood of memories for the mother, so she was telling the children how as a child she used to wade in the stream and jump into the old swimming hole and play baseball, and so on. Little Harold looked at his mother and said, "Mom, I sure wish I had met you earlier in your life."

No Perfect Parents

I feel for every young couple trying to raise children today. It takes a heap of love to live out the years of parent-child relationship and so much patience! It has been said that if we were perfect parents, we wouldn't need Jesus Christ. But there are no perfect parents! And in Jesus Christ, we know that time and time again we are driven, as caring, loving parents, to our knees because of our own need for love and forgiveness and because of our need to fulfill the yearnings of our hearts within our home.

The city of Milwaukee had an essay contest especially for boys. In response to the given title, one lad wrote, "Every child should love their father because if it were not for their fathers, where would they be? Nowhere, that's where they'd be. If it were not for fathers, you would hardly see no children in Milwaukee." That may be just about as much as some children today know about their fathers.

Robert Wells has written sensitively as a father in *To My Children, with Gratitude:*

> Yesterday we walked in the woods behind the house, shuffling through the fallen leaves, following the trail our feet had made past a fallen oak, and past the remnants of a stone wall erected by men now dead.

He stopped and waited for me while his collie blundered ahead. In the fields behind the woods a single crow flapped silently away; the wind from the west was cold.

"I like it this time, even this time of year," he said. He looked up at me and then away. "Even when I'm big . . ." he stopped; I waited, sensing that this was something I would remember. "We'll always have our woods, won't we, Dad, even when I'm big, I mean, we can come here?"

I do not lie to my children; it is a matter of pride with me to tell them the truth as best I can, even when it is hard to do so. I did not really lie to him now.

"Yes," I said, "we'll always have our woods. No matter how big you get, we will walk here like this." For we shall. The boy I love now will change into a youth who bears his name and into a man who will stroll through scuffled leaves with children of his own. And still there will be a part of him and a part of me that will walk together along the path . . . paths of fallen oaks. And while our memories last, the woods will live in us as they did the day we stood there and listened to the tick of encroaching time.

Paul says that the fifth commandment is the only one with a promise. "That thy days may be long upon the land which the LORD thy God giveth thee." He is not talking about living to an old age. Deeper than that, he is talking about *cultural survival.* If civilization, as we know it, is to continue, it will begin and reside primarily in our homes where loving respect and authority and personal relationships will be honored in the Lord.

Children, love your parents. Parents, honor your Lord. And the love learned by parents and children in the laboratory of the home will then equip you to go and love in a lonely and fragmented world.

Questions

1. How do you understand the command to "honor" your father and mother?
2. Using the biblical model in Ephesians 5:21–6:4, how would you describe family life that would be pleasing to God?
3. Using the above model and considering your own family—past or present—what strengths and weaknesses do you perceive?
4. Name at least one thing that you are committed to do to improve your own family life. If married, consider how you might "honor" your own parents or someone else's.

7

THE VALUE OF LIFE

Thou shalt not kill.

Exodus

The sixth commandment is short and succinct: "Thou shalt not kill." In the Old Testament we know that this meant: Thou shall not murder. In the New Testament, Jesus broadens the base and interprets this commandment as he does many of the others. The Old Testament refers to *action;* the New Testament's interpretation refers also to *attitude.* The Old Testament deals with deeds; the New Testament deals with the entire emotional framework from which murder and killing come. In this commandment, we are confronted with the mystery of God and ourselves and with the preciousness of life as God conceives it.

It is a complex commandment; it touches everything from mercy killing to highway deaths, to abortion, to war, to suicide, and capital punishment. The implications deal with life in our times in such breadth that it touches us all.

In these few words, we are faced with the paradox of man himself: that mankind can and does take his best—his brilliance and his skill—to wage war on viruses and germs. He does his best to sustain life and even to make life more comfortable. And then

he takes those same skills, those same energies, the
same God-given power, and develops instruments
of destruction to *take* life.

Science

In his book, *The Immense Journey,* Loren Eiseley,
a gifted scientist, traces the question of the elusive-
ness of the meaning of life. Eiseley asks a question:
"When the newsmen are in the laboratory, and the
flashbulbs pop, and we have made the great transfor-
mation of life into forms of human life, shall we,
when we think we are God himself, shall we really
have answered the question of the illusiveness of
the meaning of life? Shall we even touch," he asks,
"the plaguing question of the saw-tooth leg of a
grasshopper, the mystery of a song bird, the marvel
of man? Shall we, when we stir the slime, be able
to do the things in the laboratory—shall we know
or shall we merely push back the spectrum even further, seeking after the mystery of life itself?" In the
closing paragraph of that book, he writes:

> I do not think, if someone finally twists the key suc-
> cessfully in the tiniest and most humble house of
> life, that many of these questions will be answered
> or that the dark forces which create lights in the
> deep sea and living batteries in the waters of tropical
> swamps, of the dread cycles of parasites, or the most
> noble workings of the human brain, will be much,
> if at all, revealed. Rather I would say that if "dead"
> matter has reared up this curious landscape of fid-
> dling crickets, song sparrows, and wondering men,

it must be plain, even to the most devoted materialist, that the matter of which he speaks contains amazing, if not dreadful powers and may not impossible be, as Hardy has suggested, "but one mask of many worn by the Great Face behind."[6]

Murder

The gospel of Jesus Christ brings to focus the fact that life is more than breathing; that life, somehow, has more meaning than simply existing; that the *quality of life* is as important as the *existence of life* itself. In the Old Testament one thing is clear: thou shalt not kill a man because God, in the mystery of his creation, made man in his own image. Adam is God's image bearer and you shall not kill him, God said.

Speaking theologically, murder or the taking of another life is an assault upon the Creator. The Bible makes that clear: "Whoever sheds the blood of man, by man shall his blood be shed; for God made man in his own image" (Gen. 9:6, RSV). The destruction of another life, either in the physical fact of taking that life or by harming the spirit of a person is performing an assault on God. That sobering thought gives this commandment a deeper meaning for us.

In the Old Testament the implications were clear—murder could be done either as an act of deliberate will or it could be done as a momentary careless act of passion: "Whoever strikes a man so that he dies shall be put to death. But if he did not lie in wait for him, but God let him fall into his hand, then I will appoint for you a place to which he may flee" (Exod. 21:12–13, RSV).

From these words we get the modern concept of a "sanctuary" for persons. They may go to a church, theoretically to the altar, and be free from secular powers. Then in verse 14 we read, "But if a man willfully attacks another to kill him treacherously, you shall take him from my altar, that he may die." The Bible goes on, "When an ox gores a man or a woman to death, the ox shall be stoned, and its flesh shall not be eaten; but the owner of the ox shall be clear. But if the ox has been accustomed to gore in the past, and its owner has been warned but has not kept it in, and it kills a man or a woman, the ox shall be stoned, and its owner also shall be put to death" (21:28–29, RSV).

At first, these Old Testament passages seem contradictory. God says that if a person takes another life and breaks the commandment, "You shall not kill," then *you shall kill him!* I suggest that this is, on the surface, a contradiction. God set up severe prescriptions in the Old Testament to restrain the destructiveness of man in the willful murder of another human being. The seeming contradiction must be viewed in the context of a crude and primitive society to restrain violent acts of murder.

In our own day, we must take advantage of the whole biblical account. Let's not go back into the

Bible and take little pieces of it here and there to prove a point. That would not be treating the Scriptures with true respect. God, in his love, progressively revealed his ultimate ideal in Jesus Christ and his love.

Capital Punishment

There are some basic lessons in the two passages from Exodus that are pertinent for us, and one of them has to do with capital punishment. In that primitive society, there were no instructions of rehabilitation, no possibility of rehabilitating a murderer. The requirements consistent with that day no longer exist. Though I recognize today's controversy, it is my opinion—drawn from the Scriptures, from experience and from the love of Christ—that we can in no way justify capital punishment. For me it is a violation of God's commandment, "Thou shalt not kill."

Part of my conviction has to do with the preciousness of life, grounded in the Old and New Testaments. Beyond that is the new fact brought about by the Holy Spirit's power in Jesus Christ and the *redeemability* of a person. All one has to do is meet one person on death row—one charged to die by execution—and then discover that this person has had a wholly changed life, and is now a servant of Jesus Christ. Yet the law in its punitive aspect would be carried through to his execution.

Highway Deaths

We discover in Exodus that if an ox broke out of its pen and gored a man—which was a tragic thing—the owner could not be held responsible. But if the owner had been warned and he knew that the ox habitually broke out of its pen and he did not take precautions and the ox broke out and killed a man, not only the ox would be killed but also the owner.

All of this begins to have implications for us when we consider that the *automobile is a mechanized ox!* For the past twenty years, we have averaged over thirty-five thousand deaths per year on the highways. Recently, the figures have risen to over fifty thousand. In fifteen years, we have killed more people on the highways than the accumulation of all our wars. This commandment demands that we give more careful attention to the condition of our mechanized oxen and the laws that govern our behavior.

I ask questions like this in trying to respond to the commandment. Is it not reasonable that every mechanized ox be inspected regularly to see that it is safe? Is it not also reasonable to expect the driver to be safe? If hearing and sight and coordination are essential for safe handling of these vehicles, isn't it important that we have some periodic check-up to know whether we are still able to control them for the safety of others? Isn't it reasonable, when we know that over half of the deaths on our highways are caused by the misuse of alcohol, that we begin to be more serious about the destructive effects of alcohol, especially as it relates to drivers and drunkenness?

War

Certainly, war is the touchiest implication of the commandment, "Thou shalt not kill." It is the supremely plaguing question of our time. If anything positive came from the Vietnam War, it is that many of us, for the first time, were forced to look in depth at the obsolescence of war itself.

George Bernard Shaw reminds us of our foolishness in *Man and Superman:*

> I have examined man's wonderful inventions and I tell you that in the arts of life, man invents nothing. But, in the arts of death, he outdoes nature herself. When he goes out to slay, he carries a marvelous mechanism that lets loose at the touch of his finger all the hidden molecular energies, and leaves the javelin, the arrow, the blowpipe of his fathers far behind. His heart is in his weapons. Man measures his strength by his destructiveness.[7]

Increasingly, we measure our strength by our military might, not by our capacity to produce ideas and goods. Harry Emerson Fosdick, who wrote some of his best material in the heat of World War I, also wrote the very sensitive book, *The Unknown Soldier.* In it he writes, "Of all insane and suicidal procedures, can you imagine anything madder than this:

that all the nations should pick out their best, use their scientific skill to make certain that they are the best, and then in one mighty holocaust offer ten million of them on the battlefields of one war?"

If it were possible to feel, to see, and to sense the awesomeness of modern weaponry, I am confident we would all share the grief and the anguish of many people today. I've searched hard with this in my heart and soul, and I fully recognize the implications of some things I write here. Today our weaponry won't sort out combatants and noncombatants. Our older grenades and firepower still efficiently shatter flesh; they rip and tear people apart. But now the silos with intercontinental ballistic missiles with nuclear warheads, the great reconverted ships that can go in and level a whole area, the submarines with nuclear armed missiles have changed conventional warfare forever and their firepower and destructive potential is awesome! "Ancient man smashed skulls but we smash cities" (Chad Walsh).

In World War I, eight million people were killed. In World War II, sixteen million were killed. In World War III—it is horrendous to contemplate! A war of nuclear power would not be a war against mankind—it would be a war against God. It would be a war against children yet unborn. With the weaponry we now have in our arsenals of tens of millions of tons of TNT for every human being on the earth, there is an urgency to this commandment that ought to grip our souls and our minds. "Thou shalt not kill."

Patriotism is not necessarily rattling our weapons and building bigger arsenals. A true patriot in Jesus Christ often aches and cries, "God help us!" The only way a Christian has justified war is when, in his heart of hearts, he felt it was the lesser of two grim evils. But God forgive us for making it popular, or thinking we are patriotic to advance war. Patriots have died defending their country against what they judge is a greater evil, but except as an alternative to a greater evil, we should never condone war.

In wrestling with this problem, we turn to Jesus and struggle with his words. He moved the entire question of killing to the realm of the spirit. He said, "You've heard of old that it is wrong to murder. I say to you, don't say *Raca!* Don't say 'you fool,' or you're going to hurt a person inside" (see Matt. 5:22). Murder is more than damaging flesh. Murder, Jesus said, is also damaging to a person's spirit. We are not to do anything that diminishes another person's human personality and integrity.

Nowadays, we don't even say "raca" anymore. We don't know what it means. I suppose a close synonym might be "stupid." In recent years, it could have been "wop" or "kike" or "nigger." If Jesus had come in 1960, I think he would have made his point like this: "If any of you say to another person, 'nigger,' you are in danger of hell!"

We care about somebody mistreating our children; think how God cares. Jesus said, "You shall not harm a person inside." He went on, and it gets very tough; one comes close to the cross. "Ye have heard that it hath been said, Thou shalt love thy neighbour and hate thine enemy" (Matt. 5:43). But listen to the very next verse: "But I say unto you, *Love your enemies*" (5:44). How can we fire nuclear warheads upon those we must love? God, in Jesus Christ, says, "Children, love your enemies. Love those who despitefully misuse you personally. A new commandment I give unto you, love one another." Don't kill your enemy, love him.

Most of us are not really touched by the commandment, "Thou shalt not kill." But none of us are untouched when our Lord moves in to deal with our attitudes toward one another. God, in Jesus Christ, begins with us where we are and says, "Don't hate your enemy and don't kill him. Love him." There we come up against a cross with our will, our pride, and we come up against God's ultimate design for all of life.

I pray with all my heart that our young people will keep on singing, that God will help them sing, help them to have hope, help them to wage peace. Jesus' message comes through in words like this: "Don't keep hurting each other. Don't keep killing— either the flesh or the spirit."

Love: that is the radically tougher commandment.

Questions

1. Make a list of what you think should be considered in keeping this commandment today.
2. List the three most frequent ways this commandment is broken.
3. Choosing one from your list above, describe what you think could and/or should be done to improve our keeping this commandment.
4. State as clearly as you can what you are going to do about the area you chose in number 3.

8

YOUR PURITY
AND GOD'S LAW

Thou shalt not commit adultery.

Exodus 20:14

The seventh commandment is perhaps the most delicate of all ten. As this commandment was given in the Old Testament, it clearly was related to marriage. It called for faithfulness, saying clearly and crisply that "thou shalt not break the covenant vows you make with a partner"—that is, you shall not have sex relations with someone outside of your marriage.

When Jesus addressed himself to the law, he went beyond the fundamental meaning of the code. He dealt with the underlying conditions from which the breaking of the code comes. Jesus said, "Ye have heard that it was said by them of old time, Thou shalt not commit adultery; But I say unto you, That whosoever looketh on a woman to lust after her hath committed adultery with her already in his heart" (Matt. 5:27–28).

Beyond Marriage

Jesus digs down to our thoughts and our attitudes, and, by so doing, he moves the commandment beyond marriage vows and the marriage contract and applies it to all of life. As Jesus interprets this commandment, he builds on it to include single people and young people before marriage. It questions our lifestyles and the commitments and boundaries by which we live.

God gave us the commandments to keep us from breaking our necks and, worse yet, our hearts. So he sets a signpost, "Thou shalt not commit adultery," and that is a firm boundary. Then Jesus goes on to tell us that we are not to allow either in our thoughts or our attitudes any conditions out of which acts of adultery may flow (cf. Matt. 5:27–28).

Cecil B. DeMille was interested in biblical themes, perhaps because he was basically a religious man. He wrote in an article concerning the commandments:

> We are too inclined to think of law as the opposite of liberty. But this is a false conception. God does not contradict himself. He did not create man and then, as an afterthought, impose upon him a set of arbitrary, irritating, restrictive rules. He made man free—and then gave him commandments to keep him free. We cannot break the Ten Commandments. We can only break ourselves against them—or else, by keeping them, rise through them to the fullness of freedom under God. God means us to be free. With divine daring, he gave us the power of choice.

Jesus says the fracturing of the law of God regarding purity is based on lust. This has nothing to do with the healthy, natural sex drive; there is a God given natural attraction between male and female. However, any temptation for illicit sex must be re-

107

futed immediately to avoid entrapment. In speaking of temptation, Martin Luther is reported to have said that we couldn't be held accountable if a bird landed on our head, but we certainly were accountable if the bird built a nest there!

Love or Lust?

The thing Jesus is warning against is "anticipatory brooding." It is dangerous to play mental sexual games. Jesus knew this was a clue, a dead giveaway: lust gives away the fact that a person has lost or is losing a sense of responsible and faithful love.

In the original Hebrew, the word adultery meant spoiling that which was pure. Milk that soured could be called "adulterated." But as Jesus expressed it here, the reference is to our physical beings and that God-given, instinctual drive for sex and sexuality.

Jesus says—and this is the heart of the matter—that any acts of adulterous love are symptoms, they are clues that we are having a problem with responsible, relational love. He understood, as we are coming to understand, that promiscuity is symptomatic of our lostness.

In his teaching, Jesus always spoke to the fundamental conditions of earthly existence, the realities of our thought life. Not the acts alone, but the attitudes. He reminded us—in his own lifestyle and words—by his death, crucifixion and resurrection that God's high call is to fulfillment and to the fullest freedom through obedience to God (cf. Phil. 2:5–11).

Your Purity and God's Law

There are many prophets of doom who like to predict that we are in our last days, that judgment is just around the corner. That may be true from the standpoint of biblical history, but of great importance to us now is our need to focus our attention on the commandments and reaffirm our commitment to them today! As Christians, we need to choose, by an act of free will, to live the way of obedience to God's commandments. We feel his high call to purity, we feel the anguish of our own self-centeredness, but we know that God's call to freedom and fulfillment is found in responsible covenant behavior with God and with one another. We march to "the beat of a different drummer."

A Costly Commitment

Recently, I looked over my record book of weddings. Reading the names listed there brought back some tender memories. The youngest couple was just under eighteen years of age; the oldest in their seventies. One couple, I especially remember, after twenty-five years of marriage repeated their vows again, recommitting themselves to one another, this time with their children standing with them. I don't remember any couple I've married who didn't desire the fulfillment of the vows they made as they stood in that place of reverence in God's house. "I, John, take thee, Mary, to be my wedded wife, and I do promise and covenant before God and these witnesses to be thy loving and *faithful* husband." I hear

109

them say that and very often can sense their deep joy and commitment.

What happens at times that spoils the beauty of this kind of commitment? The answer to that is what this seventh commandment is all about—the fundamental conditions out of which come thoughts and acts. We often misuse each other in our marriage and drive each other to breaking the commandment, either in thought or act. But to become "one," to be committed to one another within the boundaries of marriage, does not violate the other's personality.

It is to be hoped that we are learning more and more to respect the personhood of another human being, female and male. This means the ability to have our own views and thoughts, and even our own lifestyle, without feeling they must be just like our partner's. In our love for our marriage partner and within the boundaries of our commitment in Jesus Christ, we are to find a new freedom for ourselves and for them. If we don't, we can injure that person and drive them into loneliness out of which may come the fracturing of this commandment.

God, then, always directs us from *lust* to *love*— to a love that gives freedom to the other person. God's love is the affirmation of the other person, with an appreciation of our differences, and the acknowledgment that the other person's views have something to offer us. The best possible way to get to know another human being is to be married—intimately, lovingly, faithfully married.

A human being is body and spirit, both at the same

time. We are so much animal that a good veterinarian can treat most of our physical problems. When we lust, we are more animal than human, but when we love truly and unselfishly, we are more like God. A veterinarian may treat my body, but only God himself can treat my spirit. That treatment is what he offers us in this commandment as an expression of his love.

Examples in Literature

According to Scripture and human experience, when adultery is committed, the offender is hurt as well as the offended. Literature is replete with examples that mirror that fact. A touching example is *Adam Bede,* a great novel by George Eliot. Hetty, the young and attractive girl, is headstrong, selfish, vain and proud. But Adam Bede loved her. He was a simple man, a carpenter, and he wanted so desperately to make her his own. Then Arthur Donnithorne, the playboy with lots of money and very little principle, ruined Hetty in one promiscuous act. A child was born, and Hetty and the child wandered the earth, agonizing, lonely, searching. Adam Bede with his steady, quiet love was there. Finally, Arthur Donnithorne came to Adam and asked his forgiveness. Adam said, "I forgive you. But sir, there is a kind of damage that can't be made up for." And there *is.*

God, in his loving way, puts up signposts to say, "If you are going to go on that way, you'll end up with a broken heart yourself." You can't violate the integrity of another person without violating your own, and you are both too precious for that.

Nathaniel Hawthorne's *The Scarlet Letter* is certainly a profound work, built on the issue of adultery. Hester had to wear the embroidered red "A" in society. Branded! Caught in adultery! But no one knew who the guilty man was. Hester carried her shame alone. But the real impact of the story comes in what happened in the lives of the people involved. Hester worked her way through to forgiveness in Jesus Christ and to a life of gentle service. Her husband, Chillingworth, became bitter. He searched hard and finally unearthed the offender. It was his friend, the minister. Chillingworth became so bitter and cynical that he died in his anger. The minister offender went through life carrying the burden of guilt and agony until finally, he, too, found the freedom of forgiveness.

Forgiveness—Where Judgment and Grace Meet

But, the good news of the gospel is that God never gives us a commandment without also telling us he loves us. To any who have fractured his commandments, he always offers forgiveness. That is where judgment and grace are one, in the Bible, and we can't experience his grace without acknowledging his judgment.

So often I have thought how fortunate most of us were in our growing-up years when we were making value judgments. At the same time, our young people today are confronted with so much unbiblical input which they must sort through in their search for real, wholesome physical love. It takes special sensitivity on the part of adults—at home, in church and school—to help a young person understand more than biology. By our words and actions, we are to give them a model of commitment and covenantal love.

For so long there was a tragic distortion in the church's teaching on "the flesh," our sexuality, the physical aspect of life. The early church was conditioned by Greek philosophical thought in which "the flesh" was considered sinful. However, Paul's teaching is clear: the flesh itself is not sinful, but it becomes sinful when sin enters the heart. In New Testament thought, the flesh becomes the "arena" that evil uses to hurt or even destroy us.

Our Bodies Are Good!

The basic Christian message to that ancient pagan and corrupt world, and to ours, was that these bodies of ours are good. They are the very places in which God chose to dwell! When God came to earth in the person of Jesus Christ, "The Word became flesh and dwelt among us" (John 1:14, RSV). The Incarnation was once and for all the answer to the question, "How does God view the body?"

Pleasure, satisfaction, and fulfillment in the realm of the physical all are a part of God's will and plan for us. He knew what he was doing when he made our sexual urges and drives. He knew, also, that unless these are fulfilled in the context of integrity, intimacy, and commitment, they are self-destructive and exploitive of others. Dr. Frank Crane writes:

> Every generation a new crop of fools comes on. They think they can beat the orderly universe. They conceive themselves to be more clever than the eternal laws. They snatch goods from Nature's store and run and one by one they all come back to Nature's counter, and pay—pay in tears, in agony, in despair; pay as fools before them have paid. Nature keeps books pitilessly. Your credit with her is good, but she collects. There is no land you can flee to and escape her bailiffs, she never forgets; she sees to it that you pay her every cent you owe, with interest.

God, just as he has set inexorable laws operating in nature, has ordered certain results in our spiritual beings as well. If we refuse to listen and to follow him, then we are broken in the process. But if we do listen to God, his grace exceeds our ability to understand it.

There is a story in our Old Testament that is both touching and sordid. It concerns Gomer, Hosea's wife. She deserted her home and husband to become a temple prostitute. As the years went by, Gomer lost her beauty and her own sense of worth. The turning point in that poignant book in the Bible comes when she was put on the block in the public market, to be sold like an animal. Hosea learned of this turn of events and went to the public market to bid for her. He bought his own wife back. He paid for her, half with grain and half with silver. When he took her home, he put his arms around her and loved her to purity again. As Hosea reflected on his own emotions, he said to himself, "If I love my Gomer this much, how much must God love us who go a-whoring after other gods?"

The Law of Love

That is the message of Jesus. That is how much he loves us. He puts his arms around us—broken, troubled, searching—and turns us around.

One day, a group of Jews caught a woman in the act of adultery. They had it all figured out; they were fine, crisp legalists. They knew the law, so they took her and threw her half-naked at the feet of Jesus. Her face was in the dirt. To test Jesus, they asked, "Rabbi, what does the law say?" They held rocks in their clenched hands, for they knew the law said she should be stoned. Jesus didn't answer their question, but instead he bent down and began writing with his finger in the dust. Scripture doesn't tell us what Jesus wrote, but it does tell us that as the woman's accusers watched him, they continued to press him for an answer.

Finally, Jesus stood up, looked at them and said, "He that is without sin among you, let him first cast a stone at her" (John 8:7). Then he stooped down again and continued to write. I'm inclined to think that at least one of the words Jesus wrote was "lust."

At any rate, John tells us that after a time the scribes and Pharisees walked away and left them alone.

Jesus then stood up, looked around, and asked the woman, "Where are those thine accusers? hath no man condemned thee?" And then she said, "No man, Lord." Now comes those magnificent words of Jesus, "Neither do I condemn thee: go, and sin no more" (John 8:10–11). Jesus never condoned her act of adultery, but he forgave her. Undoubtedly he felt confident of her repentance.

The Church—A Hospital for Sinners

It was unlikely people who made up the early church. They were tax collectors, quislings, people who hurt terribly inside because nobody would have anything to do with them. They were prostitutes, Samaritans, drunkards. But to all of these God's healing touch came time and time again. The love of Jesus set them free, and they became the people of God— the church. No wonder they sang, no wonder they loved each other, and no wonder they invited each other to share in the love of God. That's what the church is. It is a place where in our broken humanity, with our reaching out and our searching, with our adultery, our lust, we come to grips with ourselves and with each other. And we feel that high call, his loving, probing summons to purity, and to boundaries within which we can live to the fullest the pleasures of physical life, in intimacy and commitment.

The apostle Paul wrote, "I am crucified with Christ:

116

nevertheless I live; yet not I, but Christ liveth in me: and the life which I now live in the flesh I live by the faith of the Son of God, who loved me, and gave himself for me" (Gal. 2:20). Paul also wrote, "The Holy Spirit becomes the custodian of your body." Isn't it wonderful that Almighty God chooses our bodies to live in, that his Spirit wants to dwell in us? "Know ye not that ye are the temple of God, and *that* the Spirit of God dwelleth in you?" (1 Cor. 3:16). When we open our lives to God and let the Holy Spirit be the custodian of our thoughts and actions, then we will be close to what God is talking about in this commandment.

The message is clear, "Thou shalt not commit adultery," either in act or in the mind. Rather, we are to live out our physical lives in commitment to him and to those he has given us to share our lives with.

Questions

1. Describe some different understandings you think people have today about love.
2. What do you think God permits and what does God forbid in sexual behavior when he gives us this commandment?
3. Describe specifically how this commandment speaks to your own sexual behavior.
4. Explain what is most important to you in the keeping of this commandment, and name something you can do to help you continue to keep it.

9

THE PERIL IN POSSESSIONS

Thou shalt not steal.

Exodus 20:15

Let him that stole steal no more: but rather let him labour, working with his hands the thing which is good, that he may have to give to him that needeth.

Ephesians 4:28

"Thou shalt not steal" is an affirmation that all things belong to God. He is the One who created and owns the whole earth. We in turn are given free gifts by God to act as his trustee or manager of those gifts.

In Psalm 24, David says, "The earth *is* the LORD's, and the fullness thereof; the world, and they that dwell therein." And in the book of Exodus we read, "for all the earth *is* mine" (19:5). In other words, we build our thinking on this commandment from the affirmation that everything belongs to God. We come into this world without possessions, and we will leave without them, but in the interim, God has appointed us as trustees of all that is his. He places goods and persons within the circle of influence and gives us the privilege of exercising stewardship over them.

I think it is important for us to understand, though, that if we break this commandment, we not only disobey God but we also rob another person of exercising his stewardship. In other words, to break the commandment, "Thou shalt not steal," is not just a violation of God's direct order. It also violates the right of others to exercise stewardship over what God has given them.

We get an interesting insight into this through the ancient Israelites. When Moses died and Joshua took over as their leader, they moved across the Jordan into Canaan after having spent forty years wandering around in the wilderness. They were now prepared to conquer their enemies and occupy the "Promised Land." But right at the outset Joshua reminded the people of this very commandment and said, "Thou shalt take no treasured thing from your enemy." Those were his exact words. How sensitive! They were not to steal even from their enemies.

The Rich Young Ruler

Luke tells of the cautious, probing question of a young man called a "rich young ruler." He had it made. He was young, he had prestige and position in the community, and he had material wealth. But, interestingly enough, he didn't have life. The young man asked Jesus, "Good teacher, tell me, what must I do to have eternal life?" When Jesus reminded him he was to keep the commandments, his quick reply was that he had kept them from his boyhood on. Then Jesus told him to get rid of his wealth "and, come follow me." But next we read that the young man "was very sorrowful: for he was very rich" (cf. Luke 18:18–23). For him, material possessions were more important than Christ.

God says that we aren't to let our possessions so

possess us that we misuse them, and we are not to obtain them wrongly or keep them from someone who should share in them. In the commandment against stealing, God hits right at the heart of where we live in the practical things of life.

Twice in Jesus' ministry he had dramatic confrontations with publicans—tax collectors. One was Levi and the other was Zacchaeus. Although both were Jews, they were employed by the hated Roman government. And, like all tax collectors in those times, they were despised because of the common practice of collecting more than they paid Rome and keeping the difference. It was a legal form of stealing.

A Look at Levi

One day, Levi was sitting in his tax office and Jesus saw him. Even though it might have appeared to others from a material point of view that Levi had it made, Jesus knew he was a lonely and empty man. Without rebuking him, Jesus said, "Follow me." And immediately Levi left his chicanery, followed Jesus Christ and became a clean person and a disciple of the Lord and was renamed Matthew.

Zacchaeus, another tax collector, met Jesus on the streets of Jericho. He had heard Jesus was coming to town, and since he was short and couldn't see above the crowd, he climbed up in a tree and went out on a limb. What a funny place for a grown man to be! But he wanted to see the Master. When Jesus walked along the street, he stopped at the foot of the tree, looked up at the little man and told Zacchaeus to come down because he wanted to have dinner with him. Something happened when Zacchaeus met the Lord. It was a dramatic happening because Zacchaeus promised to pay back four times as much as he had stolen.

Subtle Ways of Stealing

We all struggle with this commandment. Of all the ten, I suspect this is the one most freely broken. We do it in subtle ways. Most people would be offended at the thought of stealing something of great value, but the subtle ways we steal little things are a part of the corruption that runs throughout our society. Through the years, I have clipped many news stories that point to the breaking of this commandment and I have quite a collection.

At Quonset Point, Rhode Island, during World War II the Marines were called out every time a Navy plane crashed. Why? To encircle the plane and guard it lest the local populace strip it naked. Great care has to be taken during times of disaster to prevent looting and stealing.

One of the saddest news stories I have read concerns a seventeen-year-old. He was president of his class and had already received an appointment to the Air Force Academy in Colorado. One tragic night, concerned about passing an exam, he stole the answers to the exam. The guard, not knowing who the shadowy figure was, called for him to halt. When the boy refused to stop, the guard shot and killed him. In the newspaper articles, the mother and father are quoted as saying that all the boy could think of was that appointment. He didn't want to risk failure by flunking that exam.

The parents in their grief said more than they knew—all he had in his mind was that appointment. But God wants us to have more on our minds than material gain or personal achievement. Instead, our minds are to be full of love for God. It is his desire and will for us to live honestly and with integrity.

Years ago we traded at a small butcher shop. There were times when we had the feeling that the butcher weighed his thumb along with the meat. The Bible says, almost with a touch of humor, that we are to be honest in our measures, "Thou shalt not have in thine house divers measures, a great and a small. *But* thou shalt have a perfect and just weight, a perfect and just measure shalt thou have: that thy days may be lengthened in the land which the LORD thy God giveth thee. For all that do such things, *and* all that do unrighteously, *are* an abomination unto the LORD thy God" (Deut. 25:14–16).

Bigger and Better Barns

In the New Testament, we read of Jesus' confrontation with men on their use of possessions. To one man who "had it made," who kept building bigger and bigger warehouses, the word came in a parable that in today's language might sound like this, "What good would it do you to gain it all if you are not careful how you gain it? Suppose you gain it all, and in the process lose your soul? Then what will it profit you, man?" (cf. Luke 12:16–21).

In the Old Testament, we find the story of Achan (Josh. 7). He was a member of Joshua's victorious army as they moved through Canaan. But one day he "saw among the spoils" of battle a beautiful cloak from Babylonia, two hundred shekels of silver and a solid gold bar. Achan couldn't resist the temptation. He stole the silver and gold and hid them in his tent.

Because of this theft, the army of Israel began to suffer reverses until Achan's sin was exposed. And it wasn't until punishment was meted out to Achan that things became normal again. Even today it is the cheating and stealing Achans who disturb the normal patterns of community life.

The sin of stealing has indeed plagued humankind since the dawn of time. It takes many forms—some of them very subtle. For example, the Israelites were warned, "Thou shalt not remove thy neighbour's landmark, which they of old time have set in thine inheritance, which thou shalt inherit in the land that the LORD thy God giveth thee to possess it" (Deut. 19:14). In so many words the writer is saying, "Don't move those markers around and steal each other's property." Even then there were those whose greed prompted them to such surreptitious acts as moving a survey stake on their neighbor's property. Of course, it isn't likely we would try something like that because we know it wouldn't work. But we have our own subtle ways of fudging in "little" things—even if no one else knows, God does, and so do we.

In the days when Oklahoma was an Indian territory, folks lined up at the border so that when the gun sounded for the "Great Run," they could take off and stake their claims. Some of the lush valleys, the stark barren plains and the hills had oil in the ground. Some of the folks didn't play fair and slipped over the line the night before and staked their claims before the gun went off in the morning. When the rest of the people got there, those "sooners" had already staked their claims to choice land. The nickname "sooners" was theirs because they got there *sooner* than they were supposed to.

"Thou shalt not steal" applies to cheating on income taxes, on tests, at the gas station. It applies to stealing time from employers through long coffee breaks, extended lunch hours, and doing personal business on company time. White collar crime is rampant as huge companies are accused of overcharging on service and products. Shoplifting has become a national epidemic of stealing and large corporations cheating on prices for items on government contracts are in the news daily. The question so often doesn't seem to be "Is it wrong?" but "Can we get away with it?"

For the Christian, "Thou shalt not steal" means that we are not to cut corners in either time or material gain. We respect the rights of our neighbors and even of government. And we work constantly at being good stewards of everything that God has placed in our trusteeship. This we do so as not to offend God by breaking his commandment. And this we do to preserve our own integrity and not lose our souls.

Questions

1. Discuss the biblical idea that God is Maker and Owner of all things and that man's role is meant to be a steward or manager for God on the earth.
2. Think of some things that people do that are usually not thought of as stealing but, in the light of this commandment, may well be stealing.
3. Consider things that you are doing or have done that might well be violations of God's will in your stewardship of possessions.
4. Name one thing that you are going to stop doing because you want your life to be more in conformity with the intent of this commandment.

10

TRUTH OR CONSEQUENCES

Thou shalt not bear false witness against thy neighbour.

Exodus 20:16

Pilate saith unto him, What is truth? And when he had said this, he went out again unto the Jews, and saith unto them, I find in him no fault at all.

John 18:38

There is no question that this law, when it was given, had to do with a courtroom scene and with perjury. It meant, "Thou shalt not bear false testimony against your neighbor as in a court of law." Later in the New Testament, we have Christ's explanation of God's commandment when through his words and example, he wants us to see that we are not only to tell the truth, we are to *live* the truth.

Witnesses False and True

For its day, the Old Testament law was very sophisticated. If you read the Book of Deuteronomy carefully, you gain some insight into the ancient period. For instance, a man could not have been forced in a Jewish court of law to testify against himself—particularly if that testimony could do damage to him. We wrote the same thing into the Fifth Amendment of the Constitution, and we often use that amendment today. We plead the Fifth Amendment so that we won't be forced to bear witness against ourselves. But the Hebrews went beyond that. They recognized that one witness might be malicious in intent

130

and might concoct a story out of spite. So, the Jewish law stated that there shall be at least two witnesses, preferably three, to offset the possibility of one person attempting to wrong someone else through false testimony. For example:

> A single witness shall not prevail against a man for any crime or for any wrong in connection with any offense that he has committed; only on the evidence of two witnesses, or of three witnesses, shall a charge be sustained. If a malicious witness rises against any man to accuse him of wrongdoing, then both parties to the dispute shall appear before the LORD, before the priests and the judges who are in office in those days; the judges shall inquire diligently, and if the witness is a false witness and has accused his brother falsely, then you shall do to him as he had meant to do to his brother; so you shall purge the evil from the midst of you. And the rest shall hear, and fear, and shall never again commit any such evil among you (Deut. 19:15–20, RSV).

In other words, not only was the requirement of more than one witness a safeguard, but if one was discovered to be a false witness, the punishment that would have gone to the offended or the condemned would go to the false witness. There was another subtle twist here. If more than one witness testified against a person, and the crime was substantiated and the punishment pronounced, the witnesses carried it out. These were safeguards to justice in a primitive society.

In his book, *On the Ten Commandments*, Owen Weatherly writes about the ninth commandment,

"Thou shalt not bear false witness." He makes this profound comment:

> "You shall not bear false witness against your neigh-
> bor" affirms the social aspect of man's being. To
> speak of a man as a social being is to call attention
> to the fact that a man can exist as a human creature
> only as he exists in relationship to others. These
> relationships upon which man's humanity is partially
> dependent are possible only to the extent that the
> witness men bear concerning the reality of things
> is a true one. Every deception among men weakens
> the structure of human society in which the being
> of man partly consists. This kind of sabotage of the
> community of man is what the Ninth Commandment
> expressly forbids. Emerson said, "Every lie is not
> only a suicide in the life of the liar, but it is a stab
> at the heart of society."[8]

God is saying that the basic platform of life is integrity in reality. We know that in the scientific world we have to be truthful and precise with the laws of the universe. In society, nothing is more damaging than being unable to trust and have confidence in others. And there is no greater cause for despair within a home than a fracturing of trust between family members.

Greeting False and True

Within the family setting, it is so easy to fall into a pattern of lying to one another in subtle ways. Often without knowing it, we begin to teach our children deceit in their early years. We have all known times when we made comments about a person, sometimes negative, and then the person appears and our greeting is overflowing with love and warmth. The children get the message. Or we watch a car drive up in front of the house and someone says, "Oh, no! How rude, how could they come? They didn't call. Here comes so and so!" We open the door and with great affection say, "Oh, how wonderful to see you."

We teach children deceit. I've seen it many times as I've rung doorbells and no one came. The curtains part, and an eye peeks out, but I pretend I didn't see and walk away. I remember when the child was in the room as I went in and the mother had to turn off a favorite TV program. The child became restless and finally, scowling, said to me, "Why don't you go home?" I laughed because I knew the mother was thinking the same thing! The candor of a child is refreshing and threatening, both at the same time.

Lying by Silence

On the other hand, silence can be one of the most effective lies. At times all of us are in the presence of gossip or hurtful actions which we would simply disavow if we were honest. But we keep silent. Silence is a way we lie and bear false witness.

Someone has said we should pass our words through three gates before we utter them. *First: Is it true?* If we don't know for sure that it is true, then don't repeat it. *Second: Is it helpful?* If it is not, then don't repeat it to someone else. And *Third: Is it kind?* If we would only live by these rules, there would be less hurt in the world.

There is a story told of the archbishop of Canterbury who was visiting the United States. He was warned by fellow churchmen that if he came to America he had better be careful when interviewed by reporters. They told him to be careful what he said lest he create some kind of controversy. The archbishop was known for his liberal social habits. As he was coming down the gangplank in New York harbor, a reporter said to him, "Sir, do you plan to visit the night clubs in New York?" Thinking he was being subtle, the archbishop replied, "Oh, *are* there night clubs in New York?" The next day the New York papers said, "The First Question asked by Archbishop Upon Entering the United States Is, 'Are There Any Night Clubs in New York?' "

Look for the Good

The word of the Lord comes through to us something like this, "Look for something good—something positive that will be up-building. Be real; be honest in your judgments and do not rejoice in evil." In 1 Corinthians 13, Paul says that love "rejoiceth not in iniquity, but rejoiceth in the truth." Phillips translates it, "Don't keep score of that which is evil or wrong, but look for the good and be pleased."

The story of the navigator and the ship's captain reveals how we can sometimes lie by telling the truth. The captain had no regard for the navigator. One day when making entries in the ship's log, he wrote, "the navigator took a drink today." The navigator, when he read the words, said, "Did you have to put that in there?" The captain replied in his very self-righteous way, "Well, it is the truth." The navigator was on duty during the next watch. His entry into the log read, "The captain was sober today." When the captain read that, he was furious. He confronted the navigator with it, but the navigator simply said, "Well, it is the truth."

We tell lies in many ways. Sometimes we don't even have to say a word; a cocked eyebrow says it all—or a voice inflection. At other times evasion or innuendo does the job. "Well, I'm really not free to comment on that." But you just did!

Pilate in the New Testament is a symbol of humanity and truth. He had a position of power. But one day he was confronted with Truth, face to face, and he tried to avoid the issue. He tried his best to shuttle Jesus off to someone else, but Jesus kept coming back and confronting Pilate again. Then Pilate tried to compromise—he tried to play it both ways and he couldn't do it. As he and Christ faced one another, Pilate finally asked, "People say that you are a King . . . are you a King?" Jesus said, "Thou hast said so." And he continued, "But my kingdom is not of this world. I have come to bear witness to the truth. My people hear the truth." Then Pilate said, "What is truth?"

Speaking the Truth in Love

Many times I have pondered Pilate's question, "What is truth?" And I've asked myself, what is the truth that we teach and live by today? For some of us, we have said in a hundred ways to our children that the accumulation of material goods will satisfy the lonely heart. It will not, and we know it. That is a lie. It is difficult for us to be truthful in words and actions with our children. And it often becomes more difficult as they grow up; often it is risky love that will confront with truth.

Consider the young man who had come home from Vietnam. He had been lounging around the house for six weeks without making any attempt to find a job. One day his father asked, "Son, why don't you go to work?" The young man was irritated. It was obvious that he resented his father's question. "All right," he replied, "if you want to get rid of me, I'll go to Detroit and get a job." After a brief silence, his father said, "I'll help you pack."

The boy got up and went off in a huff to his room upstairs. He stormed around, slamming doors and drawers as he packed his suitcase. The next morning he came down early for breakfast. His mother sat there gulping back the tears. She didn't know what to say. Dad sat there too, rather quietly. Finally, he asked, "Son, do you need any money?"

"No, thank you," the son crisply replied.

"Then, I'll walk you to the train." But the boy protested, "No, I'll go alone, thanks."

"I'll go with you, son," the father insisted and walked off with his boy. When they arrived at the train station, the father put out his hand and the boy responded. He gripped his father's hand quickly, said good-bye, and got on the train. As he slammed his suitcase into the rack, suddenly he realized what he was doing, and how he was acting. He ran back through the train and out to the rear platform; he called to his father, "Dad, hi, Dad . . . hi, Dad." But his father was walking slowly away with his head bowed, unable to hear his son's voice above the train noise.

His father had been willing to confront the son with the truth, in love, even in the face of rejection. That's the way God loves us. In effect, he has told us we can have the whole world but we may lose our own soul. He tells us what we are like; then he proves his love on a hill called Golgotha where we get the shock that reveals to us what we are really like and what God is like. It is then that distortion disappears and we see our real selves and we see God in his reality.

Rules to Live By

What is truth? In the closing hours of Jesus' ministry he prayed for his disciples and us, "Sanctify them

137

through thy truth: thy word is truth" (John 17:17). God's written word is our corrective. If we want to know the rules to live by—there they are. But beyond the written word is God's Son, the Living Word! He is the truth by which we are to live. And Paul says that because Jesus lives," Christ liveth in me: and the life which I now live in the flesh I live by the faith of the Son of God, who loved me, and gave himself for me" (Gal. 2:20). By his truth, his presence, we too may live.

The more we live in Jesus Christ, the more we study his Word—both written and living—the more we will know the truth. When doubt assails, we can listen to the words of the apostle Paul, "I know whom I have believed, and am persuaded that he is able to keep that which I have committed unto him against that day" (2 Tim. 1:12). And when faced with death, Paul wrote, "For we know that if our earthly house of *this* tabernacle were dissolved, we have a building of God, an house not made with hands, eternal in the heavens" (2 Cor. 5:1). That's the truth.

God commands us not to bear false witness with our lips or with our lives. To us today, this commandment comes in the words of the Master, clear-cut, probing, persuasive, *"I am the way, the truth, and the life."*

Life and truth are related. Response is called for, Jesus told us that we would know the truth and the truth would set us free. That is what we want—to be free. Free to be . . . free to live . . . free to love. And free to tell the truth.

Questions

1. What is God's chief concern in giving us this commandment?
2. How do people lie and why?
3. How do you lie and why?
4. Discuss at least one example of how you can conceive of your life in words or actions as being more truthful, and explore what you plan to do to make it so.

11

QUANTITATIVE LIVING

Thou shalt not covet your neighbour's house, thou shalt not covet thy neighbour's wife, nor his manservant, nor his maidservant, nor his ox, nor his ass, nor anything that is thy neighbour's.
Exodus 20:17

And he said unto them, Take heed, and beware of covetousness: for a man's life consisteth not in the abundance of the things which he possesseth.

Luke 12:15

We've now come to the last of the Ten Commandments: "Thou shalt not covet." In a sense, it is the basis for the breaking of all the other commandments. The impelling desire for someone else's material goods enables us to steal. Selfishness in coveting someone's wife or husband creates adultery. Greed between nations creates war. This tenth commandment, then, lays down for us the basic plank for the building of an ordered world.

We live today in the jet age—and a *get* age. We have almost obliterated the time zones. A person can have two breakfasts now as he flies from one coast to the other. We are but one sunset away from every other human being on the earth. How ironic it is that we walk today on the moon, yet we cannot find the ways to walk in peace on our streets, on the earth, or to our neighbor's. We have become a world neighborhood, but we have not become neighbors. It would appear that some want everything their neighbor has—except his friendship.

Covetousness Is Common

The Scriptures gives us an incident in the life of Christ that relates to this commandment (Luke 12:13–

15). One day a young man came to the Master and asked him to arbitrate a family dispute. He wanted Jesus to force a brother to divide an inheritance with him. Since it was common practice in those days for a rabbi to settle such an argument, this was a quite natural request. But Jesus responded, "Man, who made me a judge or a divider over you?" Then Jesus shifted the direction of the conversation, as he often did, and put his finger on the real problem; "Take heed, and beware of covetousness." He reminded us that, "A man's life does not consist in the abundance of things he possesses" (cf. Luke 12:13–15).

The other commandments said, "Thou shalt not kill," "Thou shalt not steal," "Thou shalt not lie"— all are specific and deal with an overt act. But this tenth commandment goes deeper. It has directly to do with the attitudes and emotions that produce our actions.

A Paraphrased Parable

Immediately after the conversation with the young man who asked for help with the inheritance, Jesus told a parable as an illustration. Let me paraphrase it in modern language.

A man walking in the fields one day was pleased with the productivity of his land. The man said, "Look at the way that wheat produces." So he planted more. And then he mused, as any good businessman might, "I don't have barns big enough for all this wheat." He began to center his energies and his time on building barns and got all caught up in it. Suddenly, like a chilling breeze, the word came to him: "Tonight thy soul is going to be required of thee." And on its heels, a frightening kind of question: "What good will it do you, man, if you gain the whole wide world and lose that soul?" (cf. Luke 12:16–21).

I know that in the new translation, and in most people's minds, is the thought that this man was going to die—that he felt the chill, cold wind of death. It is fair to say that God's understanding of death is more profound than ours. What Jesus was saying in this parable was that a man can *die* and go right on living. When a man loses his soul, when he lets *things* get in the way of *people and God,* he's dead already.

There is the legend on one man's tombstone, "Died, age 38; buried, age 76." When a man begins to center his life, his energies, and his thoughts on gaining more and more *things,* God reckons that that man is already dead—inside, where it counts—in his soul.

There are two things that were not wrong in the man's endeavor. It wasn't his desire. That was God-given. In fact, from the parables of Jesus comes the impression that it's God's holy desire for us to take the goods—the stuff of this universe—and develop them. Man was not merely permitted to do that in the garden scene, but was commanded to: "Replenish the earth; to bring it under subjection—to manage it as a steward of the Lord." A man was judged harshly if he took his talents and buried them in the ground. It was not pleasing to the master when the man wouldn't take any risks, but kept everything simply safe and secure.

The Selfhood of the Soul

There is nothing wrong with productivity. It is God-commanded. There was nothing wrong with building bigger barns. That may be a wise thing to do for storage purposes. The problem came when the man addressed his inner self and said, "Self—soul—take your ease. Let's just lean back and enjoy life." He didn't notice that all around him was a sea of need and a world of discovery. Jesus said that the man was in danger right at that point. Danger of what? Danger of losing his *self*—his selfhood—his *soul*.

Impulses are neither good nor bad. Wealth and prosperity are neither good nor bad. Impulses are like the keys on a piano—some black, some white. It is the *arrangement* that determines whether you have dissonance or whether you have harmony.

God has three questions to ask of the prosperous person: *How* did you gain your wealth? What has happened to *you* since you gained it? And, what are you *doing* with it? In itself, to be affluent is neither good nor bad. It can provide great opportunities for service unless you are locked into it, somehow, and got lost in the process. Then it can be demonic.

The Self Confronts Satan

Helmut Thielicke reminds us that Satan never gives his calling card when he comes. He never announces his coming. He usually comes to us with entertaining thoughts—something pleasurable. Then one day we wake up and find out we are empty, lonely and lost. What good will it do if you gain the whole wide world and lose your *self*, the very center of your being—your soul?

In this age of technology, since the industrial revolution, our economy is based upon the miraculous way in which we can supply man's wants and meet his needs. At the same time, in the spiral of supply and demand, we have to create new and fresh wants all the time to keep the system going. On the one hand, we spend billions of dollars on productivity, and, on the other, we match that with more billions to create desire on the part of persons to buy. One basic and interesting problem in the labor and management area is that items produced by industry and then advertised to the workman succeed in persuading the worker he ought to own what he has participated in making. The workman wants to buy them; and he *wants* the money to do so.

It has been suggested that one hundred years ago John Doe, if he were asked, had about seventy-two *wants*. If pressed, he might list about sixteen basic *necessities*. In the light of modern-day advertising, in today's spiraling economy John Doe has about 487 *wants*, about 94 of which are absolute *necessities*. One hundred years ago, with a limited sales force and no television, there were approximately two hundred objects that were pressed on the populace for sale. Today there are thirty-two thousand items. If you name all the brands, different varieties of the same products, the total is something like three hundred and sixty thousand.

When a person becomes bogged down in his desire for more and more things to make him happy, he runs into a wilderness. We begin to lose our own selfhood, our identity. No one would suggest, therefore, that we close down our assembly lines. Instead, we should put material things in the perspective where they belong and begin to recognize Jesus' words—that a man's happiness does not consist in the abundance of his possessions.

Although it has been unnerving at times to have our young people making their protesting noises, they are a living reflection of a prior generation that was preoccupied with material things. These young people are now trying to tell us that persons are more important than production, that life does not consist in the acquiring of goods. People are important. They are to Jesus Christ.

Of Birds, Barns and Lilies

In colorful and picturesque language, Jesus reminded his listeners one day, "Look at the birds of the air: they neither sow nor reap nor gather into barns, and yet your heavenly Father feeds them. . . . Consider the lilies of the field, how they grow; they neither toil nor spin; . . . even Solomon in all his glory was not arrayed like one of these" (Matt. 6:26–30, RSV).

It is an ironic twist that we will spend our energy, our time and our efforts to accrue enough money to buy a quiet place in the country to enjoy the birds, the trees and the flowers that we had all along—free! In our hectic pace, we go off to Bermuda, to Nassau and to Florida, Arizona and California to get back to the sun and sand and sea that God gave us—free!

Listen again to the words of Jesus as a paraphrase: "Consider the birds! Will you stop for a moment and look at the birds? Look at the flowers. Look at the crocuses and the lilies of the field. Look for a moment at what God gives you—*free.* They don't run around like you do, so anxious and fretting all the time. Yet God cares for them in beauty—things that even Solomon didn't have."

Bigger and Better—or Finer?

With tenderness almost beyond words, he says in the most loving way, "Little flock, don't you know that it is God's purpose to give you the kingdom?" What a beautiful thought. God's loving purpose in painting the crocuses, pushing them up through the hard earth and in putting rods and cones in these eyes, was *for us to see* and behold and to sing his praises. And we go on with *things,* losing *persons* in the process. "Don't you know that God wants to give us the kingdom?" We have heard Jesus' alternative to this rat race and we agree with it intellectually. We say, "Yes, Lord, that's right," but often we don't act on it.

All of this God has given us without any effort on our part. And yet, in our desire for more and bigger and better, we become so anxious and frantic that we miss the finer things in life that God has for us—free.

A Singer and Her Soul

Opera singer Jenny Lind quit in the middle of her successful career. One day a friend found her on an isolated beach. Jenny, in the dusk of the day, was leaning against a tree with an open book in her lap, seeming to brood. The friend walked up to her and asked, "Jenny, why did you quit at the time everyone seemed to love you and be with you?"

"Well," Jenny replied, "I'll admit that the plaudits of the audience were very rewarding. I found the stimulation exciting. But as I went on in my frantic activity, I found I had less time for that," waving her hand toward the beauty of the sunset, "and not time for this," indicating the open Bible in her lap.

That, I think, is where we are. We need more time for *this* as Miss Lind put it. Jesus has the final word, "And he said unto them, Take heed, and beware of covetousness: for a man's life consisteth not in the abundance of the things which he possesseth" (Luke 12:15). And right in the middle of the Sermon on the Mount, Jesus said, "But seek first his kingdom and his righteousness, and all these *things* shall be yours as well" (Matt. 6:33, RSV).

And God can trust you with them then. They won't hold you captive then.

Questions

1. How much more of what would it take to make you happy?
2. How would you describe the difference between wholesome wants and desires, and coveting? Discuss how modern advertising affects both.
3. Is there anything in your life you would now classify as coveting in the sense of this commandment?
4. Explore the difference it would make in your life if you more seriously coveted the spiritual gifts of God (1 Cor. 12) rather than anything of a material nature.

12

THE COMMANDMENT THAT FULFILLS THEM ALL

Then one of them, which was a lawyer, asked him a question, tempting him, and saying, Master, which is the great commandment in the law? Jesus said unto him, Thou shalt love the Lord thy God with all thy heart, and with all thy soul, and with all thy mind. This is the first and great commandment. And the second is like unto it, Thou shalt love thy neighbour as thyself. On these two commandments hang all the law and the prophets.

Matthew 22:35–40

I am thankful that the whole complex struggle of understanding God's will for us through the Ten Commandments was summarized for us by Jesus Christ, once and for all. In response to the young attorney's question in Matthew 22, Jesus said, "Thou shalt love the Lord thy God with all thy heart, and with all thy soul, and with all thy mind. . . . And . . . Thou shalt love thy neighbour as thyself." And then he added the line, "On these two commandments hang all the law and the prophets." What a tremendous summary of God's sovereign will for us! We are to act out our obedience to him by loving!

In 1890, a book entitled *The Greatest Thing in the World,* by Henry Drummond, appeared and became a best seller. It concerned love. In the late 1950s, another book appeared, written by Dr. Smiley Blanton, entitled *Love or Perish.* Dr. Blanton was a staff psychiatrist at Marble Collegiate Church, New York. Between 1890 and 1950, we moved into the nuclear age, and now we have within our grasp the power to destroy all life on earth. Love has become an urgent requirement for survival.

The Commandment That Fulfills Them All

Law or Grace?

God in his love has given us a law. And that law became a standard by which we might live. But the Bible makes a distinction between law and grace. In the New Testament, it is clear in the writings of the apostle Paul that the person who desires to be committed to God must still make this choice: to live by law, or to live by grace.

Paul suggests that these can become incompatible when separated. He insists in his epistles to the Galatians, Ephesians and Romans that we can make an error by trying to live by law apart from grace. In a sense, living by law without grace is a way of trying to put God in our debt. Paul words it in this way, "For by grace you have been saved through faith; and this is not your own doing, it is the gift of God—not because of works, lest any man should boast. For we are his workmanship, created in Christ Jesus for good works, which God prepared beforehand, that we should walk in them" (Eph. 2:8–10, RSV).

In our flip way we can check ourselves off against the Ten Commandments, "I do not steal; I do not kill; I don't commit adultery." And by so doing we are saying in effect, "Father, you ought to love me. I am much better than so many other people."

Christ's Obedience, Not Ours

But Paul reminds us that while the law is a standard by which we can learn to live, it is not a justifying principle with God. With deep insight, he says it is not our obedience to the law that makes us acceptable to God, but rather it is Christ's obedience to the law. Our salvation comes through the recognition of our own sin, and the love of God in Christ that was lived out in his obedience. Paul puts it this way:

> Have this mind among yourselves, which is yours in Christ Jesus, who, though he was in the form of God, did not count equality with God a thing to be grasped, but emptied himself, taking the form of a servant, being born in the likeness of men. And being found in human form he humbled himself and *became obedient* unto death, even death on a cross. Therefore God has highly exalted him and bestowed on him the name which is above every name, that at the name of Jesus every knee should bow, in heaven and on earth and under the earth, and every tongue confess that Jesus Christ is Lord, to the glory of God the Father (Phil. 2:5–11, RSV).

It is God's love and Christ's obedience that is primary, not our obedience to the law. To put it another way, how sad it would be if our children came in and out of the family by virtue of their behavior. Our children will have those days when they are just plain hard to get along with, but if the family were broken every time someone steps out of obedience, how sad that would be! We say to our children, "When you disobey, you make us unhappy and you do affect our fellowship—but you do not affect our relationship."

God says to us in Jesus Christ that our relationship with him has been settled. The fellowship may be something of a constant "homework" situation, but we don't fall in and out of the kingdom by our performance.

The Law—A Looking Glass

In his epistle to the Galatians, Paul anticipated that some people might misunderstand this. After all, if the law is not the standard by which we are accepted by God, then why have the law? Paul gives some excellent reasons why God gave the law. In Romans, he said the law is a mirror for us, "I should not have known what it is to covet if the law had not said, 'You shall not covet'" (7:7, RSV). The law, rightly understood, is like a looking glass projecting our image back to us, exposing our own selfishness. We may go right on coveting, but because of the law, we are now bothered. And this is particularly true as we see through Jesus' teaching that attitudes as well as actions reflect our disobedience and selfishness.

Further thoughtful reflection helps us understand that God set the law in the middle of a disorderly society, the way red lights are put on street corners—not because there is anything righteous about red lights, but because red lights bring order out of chaos in a selfish society. Paul says that's what God's law does. In a self-centered society, God set the law: Thou shalt not steal; thou shalt not kill.

The Law—A Tutor

In Galatians 3, Paul says the law is even more than a mirror; it is a tutor to bring us to Jesus Christ as Savior. And it is through a relationship with Christ, which transcends law, that we experience a changed life through his grace and love.

Saul of Tarsus is an excellent example of this. Though very religious, Saul was a mean man. He was deeply concerned about the legal aspect of the code. He was a student of Rabbi Gamaliel and prided himself upon his great heritage of learning. Saul not only knew the law, he kept it. In fact, he prided himself on keeping it, but he was still a mean man. Saul was there when Stephen, the first martyr of the church, was stoned. When Stephen died, he didn't vilify the crowd. Instead, the Bible says Stephen's face shone brightly as he asked God to forgive his killers. Undoubtedly, that sight affected Saul deeply. He had never before seen love like that. Law and order he had seen, but love like that? No!

Next, we pick up Saul's story when he was on his way to arrest the Christians in Damascus. It was on that road that he had a dramatic meeting with Jesus. And it was by forgiving grace that Saul became the apostle Paul. Now he understood the difference between living by a legalistic code and living by grace. From then on, Paul took his message of grace and love across the world.

Fulfilling the Law

Before his conversion, Paul thought he had to keep the law in order to be saved. After his confrontation with Jesus Christ, he came to realize a person has to be saved in order to keep the law. Only in the free love of Jesus Christ are we able to fulfill the law. What law? The law of love. That sums it all up. Jesus gave us the word that all the law and the prophets are based on this law of love. And it is this law that keeps us from disobeying all the others.

God's good news is for all of us. Whatever our backgrounds, our shortcomings, we start with the fact of God's gracious love and his acceptance of us as we are. Many of us struggle right at that point because we cannot accept ourselves—and so we cannot understand how God could accept us. But God tells us over and over, "I love you." Paul Tillich said that salvation is based on the "acceptance of God's acceptance."

God so loved the unredeemed world that he gave his only Son, that whosoever believes in him, who accepts his gift, might not perish, but might have everlasting life (cf. John 3:16). John expressed it in his first letter, "We love because he first loved us." That God first loved us is the starting place of our love.

Love Is Action

It is important for us to understand, though, that our love has a focus; it is not just an emotion. Love is not just a warm, tender feeling; it is *action*. There are four words in Greek for "love": *eros,* sensual love; *philia,* filial love; *storge,* a parent's love; and *agape,* God's love. *Agape* was a new word because it described for the first time a new love—God's love. It isn't a feeling! Jesus doesn't say we are to *like* our enemies; he says we are to *love* them.

Paul defines that kind of love when he writes that love is patient, kind, longsuffering, doesn't keep score on evil and is glad when someone succeeds. Then he goes on to say that he can be very religious, give everything he has away, be a martyr, and even have mountain-moving faith, but without love, he is nothing (cf. 1 Cor. 13).

The most profound fact concerning the commandments is that what God commands, he gives. God's gift is himself, not a code of ethics. The very love commanded becomes his greatest gift—his Son. In Christ, we can walk by God's standard; we can be restrained from evil; we can do the good that God wants.

One time Paul called himself "the chief of sinners." He knew his behavior was still not what it ought to be, but he had a direction. He pressed on toward the mark God had for him, and he said, "I live; yet not I, but Christ liveth in me: and the life which I now live in the flesh I live by the faith of the Son of God" (Gal. 2:20).

The Commandment That Fulfills Them All

This means that we can love where before we didn't even care. God teaches us to care because it is his care through us. We can break the bottleneck between us and an unloving society when we know that love and begin to exercise it and focus it upon God, neighbor, self and even our enemies. We will then fulfill all the law and the prophets, for that is what it is all about.

Questions

1. What have you learned about love?
2. How do you understand the relationship between God's commandments and God's love?
3. What have you done, or refrained from doing, by reading this book?

Notes

1. Edwin Markham, *Modern Religious Poems* (New York: Harper and Row, 1964), p. 280.
2. W. H. Auden, "For the Time Being: A Christmas Oratorio." © 1944, renewed 1972 by W. H. Auden. Reprinted from *W. H. Auden: Collected Poems,* ed. Edward Mendelson, by permission of Random House.
3. Peter L. Berger, *A Rumor of Angels* (Garden City, N.Y.: Doubleday and Co., 1969), p. 120.
4. Maltbie D. Babcock, "This Is My Father's World."
5. Elton Trueblood, *Your Other Vocation* (New York: Harper and Brothers, 1952), p. 99.
6. Loren Eiseley, *The Immense Journey* (New York: Random House, 1946), p. 210.
7. George Bernard Shaw, "Man and Superman," in *Seven Plays* (New York: Dodd, Mead, and Co., 1961), p. 619.
8. Owen M. Weatherly, *The Ten Commandments in Modern Perspective* (Atlanta: John Knox Press, 1961), p. 135.